Our Sermon For Today

Is MAD—that crazy, mixed-up magazine—really MORAL?

YOU
BETTER BELIEVE
IT!

(OR MAY LIGHTNING STRIKE YOU DOWN!)

Turn the page
and read on, pilgrim!
—Rev. Alfred E. Neuman

MAD Humor from SIGNET

by Don Martin

☐ **MAD'S DON MARTIN BOUNCES BACK** (#Q6294—95¢)
☐ **MAD'S DON MARTIN COOKS UP MORE TALES**
(#Q6295—95¢)
☐ **MAD'S DON MARTIN COMES ON STRONG** (#Y6854—$1.25)

by David Berg

☐ **MAD'S DAVE BERG LOOKS AT OUR SICK WORLD**
(#Y7014—$1.25)
☐ **MAD'S DAVE BERG LOOKS AT THE U.S.A.** (#Y6978—$1.25)
☐ **MAD'S DAVE BERG LOOKS AT MODERN THINKING**
(#Q6630—95¢)
☐ **MAD'S DAVE BERG LOOKS AT THINGS** (#T5070—75¢)
☐ **MY FRIEND GOD** (#Y6976—$1.25)
☐ **ROGER KAPUTNIK AND GOD** (#Y8153—$1.25)

by William Gaines

☐ **GOOD 'N' MAD** (#Q6342—95¢)
☐ **GREASY MAD STUFF** (#Q6499—95¢)
☐ **HOPPING MAD** (#Q6291—95¢)
☐ **MAD POWER** (#Y6741—$1.25)
☐ **THE PORTABLE MAD** (#Y6742—$1.25)
☐ **SELF-MADE MAD** (#Y6981—$1.25)
☐ **THE THREE RING MAD** (#Y6917—$1.25)
☐ **THE VOODOO MAD** (#Q6245—95¢)

THE MAD MORALITY

OR
THE
TEN COMMANDMENTS
REVISITED

Vernard Eller

A SIGNET BOOK from
NEW AMERICAN LIBRARY
TIMES MIRROR

Published by arrangement with Abingdon Press.

 SIGNET TRADEMARK REG. U.S. PAT. OFF. AND FOREIGN COUNTRIES
REGISTERED TRADEMARK—MARCA REGISTRADA
HECHO EN CHICAGO, U.S.A.

SIGNET, SIGNET CLASSICS, MENTOR, PLUME, MERIDIAN AND NAL BOOKS *are published by The New American Library, Inc., 1633 Broadway, New York, New York 10019*

FIRST PRINTING, JANUARY, 1972

6   7   8   9   10   11   12   13

PRINTED IN THE UNITED STATES OF AMERICA

Harken, Disciples of **MAD!**

This Signet edition of THE MAD MORALITY is an authorized version of the $3.79 book published by Abingdon Press.

DISCLAIMER I

The staff of **MAD** magazine (75c cheap) takes no responsibility for this book. We are happy doing our thing, namely, cluttering up the newsstands; and it didn't particularly overjoy us to find an egghead-type theologian trying to make something of it. Criticism we can take; praise from his kind could kill us.

So we want to take this opportunity to assure our readers that **MAD** (75c cheap) has no intention of upgrading its stuff. We reject the insinuation that anything we print is moral, theological, nutritious, or good for you in any way, shape, or form. We live in the midst of a corrupt society and intend to keep on making the best of it.

We gave Eller permission to use some of our old used garbage in this book, but this was principally to prove that all the good things he has said about **MAD** are definitely untrue. You can always read a genuine copy of **MAD** (75c cheap) to help take away the moral flavor of Eller's prettyfied version.

WILLIAM M. GAINES, Publisher
and ALBERT B. FELDSTEIN, Editor

DISCLAIMER II

The officials of Abingdon Press (since 1789), publishers of *The Interpreter's Bible* and the finest works of modern religious scholarship, wish to state that their publication of this book in nowise is to be construed as approval of **MAD** magazine (or even acknowledgment that it exists). Indeed, it galls us no end that the so-called "publishers" of **MAD** are getting filthy rich while our holy, pious, edifying, inspiring, enlightening publications go begging. Far be it from us to do anything to encourage this sort of **MAD**ness.

However, one of our pious virtues—among others—is tolerance of all points of view. And when Dr. Eller (who we took to be a competent scholar) called our attention to **MAD** (we had never heard of the magazine), we assumed that he knew what he was talking about and let him write this book. Then it was too late to back out. We trust that the patrons of Abingdon Press will be big enough to overlook this unfortunate situation, and will understand that **The MAD Morality** does not represent our desire to change the high-class character of Abingdon publications.

We also promise that hereafter we will investigate very carefully any and all suggestions made by the so-called Reverend Doctor Eller.

Abingdon Press

DISCLAIMER III

Come on, you guys. I never did say **MAD** was so all-fired great. I wouldn't even read the thing except my kids keep dragging it home—and a lot of people have to read a copy to get 75c worth out of it.

All in the world I ever said was that when **MAD** sets out to publish "garbage," it often comes out tasting better than the stuff most publishers peddle as "food." But this certainly is no compliment to **MAD**; they can't even do their own thing well enough to produce pure, unadulterated garbage. The fact that other publishers can do a *better* garbage job without even trying shows just how far short the **MAD** effort really falls.

And the truth is that Abingdon begged and begged and begged me for a book—and I believe in giving a publisher what he deserves and pays for. And for that matter, if you think that being author of *this* book is going to advance my reputation as a scholar and theologian, you've got another think coming.

I only wrote this book as a favor to you guys—for all the thanks I get.

Vernard Eller, B.A.,
B.D., M.A., Th.D.
Professor of Religion

CLAIMER I

It should be obvious to any clod that all three previous disclaiming parties are devout worshipers . . . of the Almighty Dollar. The whole thing is a scheme to take advantage of innocent **MAD** readers—and not-so-innocent Abingdon readers.

And, in conclusion, I protest the fact that this dull book is now being sold in a Signet mass-market paperback and thus taking advantage of EVERYBODY!

ALFRED E. NEUMAN

THE TEN COMMANDMENTS - REVISITED

PRODUCED BY: MAX BRANDEL

PHOTOS BY: U.P.I. & WORLD WIDE

I

THOU SHALT HAVE NO OTHER GODS BEFORE ME.

II
THOU SHALT NOT MAKE UNTO THEE ANY GRAVEN IMAGE.

III
THOU SHALT NOT TAKE THE NAME OF THE LORD, THY GOD, IN VAIN:

IV
REMEMBER THE SABBATH DAY: TO KEEP IT HOLY.

V
HONOR THY FATHER AND THY MOTHER:

VI
THOU SHALT NOT KILL.

VII
THOU SHALT NOT COMMIT ADULTERY.

VIII
THOU SHALT NOT STEAL.

Form 1040

U.S. Indiv

for the year January 1

1966, ending ....

▼ First name and initial (If joint return, use first names and

Please print or type

Home address (Number and street or rural route)

City, town or post office, and State

▲ Enter the name and address used on your ret
give reason. If changing from separate to jo

IX
THOU SHALT NOT BEAR FALSE WITNESS
AGAINST THY NEIGHBOR.

X

THOU SHALT NOT COVET THY NEIGHBOR'S WIFE.

INTRODUCTION

> *And Moses turned, and went down from the mountain with the two tables of the testimony in his hands, tables that were written on both sides; on the one side and on the other were they written. And the tables were the work of God, and the writing was the writing of God, graven upon the tables. When Joshua heard the noise of the people as they shouted, he said to Moses, "There is a noise of war in the camp." But he said, "It is not the sound of shouting for victory, or the sound of the cry of defeat, but the sound of singing that I hear." And as soon as he came near the camp and saw the calf and the dancing, Moses' anger burned hot, and he threw the tables out of his hands and broke them at the foot of the mountain.*
>
> —Exodus 32:15-19

It's true! It's in the book! Moses, the very first person to see the Ten Commandments, immediately got mad and broke them in disgust—smashed them to smithereens. Nobody since has done a more thorough job of it.

But the situation calls for more attention. Moses' disgust was just the opposite of ours; he was disgusted not with the commandments, but with the behavior of the children of Israel. We get disgusted with the commandments because we *want* to behave like the children of Israel. All of us at times have wished we could join Moses in demolishing those stone tablets; then we wouldn't have to worry about breaking the commandments in the other sense of the term.

But are the Ten Commandments all that bad? Perhaps we have not given them a fair hearing; after all, the spokesmen of the people to whom they were originally given, that is, the writers of the Old Testament, considered them to be God's greatest gift to man. How does that figure?

We tend to see the Ten Commandments as repressive, negative, binding, limiting. They obstruct our freedom, hold us back, keep us from having any fun, crush our flowering little personalities. That we see them so is largely our own problem—because we never have really experienced what it means to be squelched and oppressed. But the children of Israel knew; they had just been freed out of slavery.

The people who were gathered at Mt. Sinai to receive the Ten Commandments represented a group that had lived as slaves of the Egyptians for hundreds of years—much longer than the black man had to endure slavery in America. Also, their lot was harder, their suffering more intense, and their situation much more hopeless than ever was the case with American slaves.

And then, quite without warning and by sheer miracle, as it were, this God Yahweh came along, turned these people loose, and kept their former owners from getting at them. These were the people who received the commandments. The one, central, overwhelming fact of their existence was that they were *free* men—and, thanks to Yahweh, having gotten that way, they intended to stay that way.

This is the only proper background against which to understand the Ten Commandments. And we are not left to guess on this matter; the commandments themselves set the stage. We ought not to think that the Ten Commandments begin with Commandment #1; the preceding verse is the most important of all. Exodus 20:2 reads: "I am Yahweh your God, who brought you out of the land of Egypt, out of the house of bondage."

Yahweh is saying in effect: "You are free men, right?"

"Right!"

"And it took me to get you that way, right?"

"Right!"

"I have rather adequately demonstrated that your freedom is my prime concern, right?"

"Right!"

"And having done what I did, I have proved myself to be the world's leading expert on freedom, right?"

"Right!"

"Fine! Then let old Yahweh give you a few helpful tips on how to be free men and stay that way, OK?

"You people don't know it, but you stand in danger of losing your new freedom. No, it is not that the Egyptians are about to repossess you; I took good care of them. But in the first place, there are a lot of other gods around here who would dearly love to have you sign on with them. They will make you big promises about the freedoms they have to offer. But be careful! I've already proved that I am the God of Freedom, right?"

"Right!"

"What these gods offer as freedom always turns out to be slavery—that's why they are *false* gods. One God frees men; any other god enslaves men—that's the difference between the true God and false gods. Therefore . . . *you free men shall have no other gods besides me,* right?"

"Right!"

"In the second place, there are a lot of 'free' people around who will make free in inviting you to join them in setting up graven images. They carve figures of animals or of men or of the sun and moon to use in their worship. But whenever any object commands more attention, service, or homage—more of yourself—than it actually deserves, that is slavery . . . just as you had to give your Egyptian overlords more of yourselves than they justly could claim. Is that right?"

"Right!"

"So . . . *you free men shall not make for yourselves a graven image,* right?"

Etc. through Commandments #3, 4, 5, 6, 7, 8, 9, and 10.

Well, that all sounds very nice; but you can't deny that the Ten Commandments have all these knots in them: "You shall *not* do this. You shall *not* do that. You shall *not* do the other." They are as *negative* as all get out.

But that can be taken as an indication that they are guarantees of freedom!

Say that again?

Absolutely. The negativity of the commandments marks off small areas into which free men ought not go—precisely so that they can remain free to roam anywhere else in the great wide world. Consider a *positive* command, such as: You shall always leave a school building through a red painted door. Over against that put the negative command: You shall not leave school buildings through red painted doors. Which command frees more kids to get out of more school buildings more of the time? Obviously, a negative command can prohibit one action, precisely in order to free one for a host of others, whereas the positive requirement can force one into a given course of

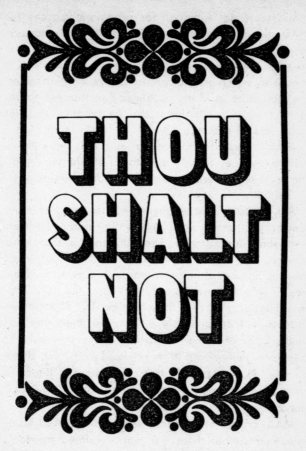

THOU SHALT NOT

action and deny him the possibility of all others. If the Ten Commandments are correct in spotting the threats to human freedom, then the negativity of their wording is indeed the invitation for man freely to find whatever style of life suits him—as long as he avoids these few pitfalls that would destroy his freedom altogether.

MAD magazine shows at least something of the same understanding of freedom that the Ten Commandments do. Although for pragmatic reasons the **MAD** men might be inclined to deny it, their magazine is dedicated to helping kids become free and stay free. In one sense, all good humor and satire is a means by which people can rise above the pettinesses, the stupidities, and the injustices that threaten to enslave them. Once a threat can be laughed at, it is much less of a threat.

MAD is dedicated to freedom, and kids sense this—that is why they rush to read the stuff. The very reading gives one a certain sense of freedom. Right?

"Right!"

But, it must be said, there are also a lot of other magazines that are dedicated to the cause of freedom —*Playboy*, for instance. The difference is that **MAD** shares a secret with the Ten Commandments of which *Playboy* has heard never so much as a whisper. *Playboy's* concept of freedom is to discard the Ten Commandments, not use them. Either by direction or indirection, there probably is not one of the commandments the breaking of which *Playboy* does not advocate. When, both in its ads and in its text, cheek by jowl, *Playboy* plumps both fast cars and liquor, it even forfeits its right to get serious about "You shall not kill."

MAD, on the other hand, sees, with the Ten Commandments, that there are many vaunted freedoms which in fact lead to slavery. The difference is that the Ten Commandments, upon seeing these, warn against them, while **MAD** makes fun of them. Both are effective means of showing up falsity. **MAD'S** satire would not come off as successfully as it does were it not coming close to the truth about the falsity which it ridicules. Satire succeeds only when it carries a good-sized load of truth.

Free men get that way and stay that way by steering clear of fake freedoms. Both the Ten Commandments and **MAD** understand this; and the very fakes that the commandments warn against are those that **MAD** ridicules. If you don't believe that, then just stick with us.

PAUL FABB

ANSWERS 20 NOSEY QUESTIONS

Here are the Questions you've been dying to ask the Georgeous, Kissable Recording Star!

What is your pet peeve?

I hate it when people who are jealous of my success accuse me of being too self-important and acting like God or something. I am not like that at all.

Where were you born?

In Pennsylvania. In a little town called Bethlehem. In a manger.

Describe yourself.

I am six feet and 175 pounds of solid, rippling muscle. I have brown, wavy hair, blue, psychedelic eyes, and when I smile, the corners of my mouth crinkle boyishly and my entire body radiates excitement, health, and fantastic virility.

What do you think is your strongest personality trait?

My humility.

What do you consider to be the most catastrophic day of the 20th Century?

November 22, 1963.

A lot of people feel the same way.

I really appreciate it. That was the day I lost my comb.

Speaking of combs, when did you take your last haircut?

In the Summer of 1953.

When did you take your last bath?

In the Spring of 1952.

What do you admire most in a person?

Neatness.

Did you study singing in school?

No, they wouldn't let me sing in school.

You were a listener?

They wouldn't let me listen either.

How did this experience affect your career as a pop singer?

Very well. I don't bring any bad habits into my music. Like rhythm, melody, harmony, and the rest of that junk.

How much money do you earn?

A million dollars a week.

Has your life changed much since you became successful?

Not at all. I always made a million dollars a week.

Always?

Yeah, I had this crazy allowance set-up at home.

How do you relax?

I like to sit around naked and count my money.

Now that you made it big, what kind of home did you set up for the people you owe so much to—your parents?

Who?

What is most important when you meet a girl—her looks or her personality?

Oh her personality, definitely. While I like a girl to be attractive, I don't think attractiveness always expresses itself in physical beauty. Even a girl who doesn't have what might be considered outstanding features can be attractive if she has enthusiasm and warmth and if she radiates a kind of inner attractiveness from her soul.

What do you enjoy doing most on a date?

Making out.

What do you consider to be the most thrilling moment in your fantabulous show business career?

The time this girl with loads of personality walked into my dressing room, locked the door, and took off all of her

(CONTINUED ON PAGE 299)

25

How different our lives are, Egbert. Look what I've got: A disturbed son with a father who never married me, 38 unwashed beatnik friends, 71 Henry Miller books and 112 Lenny Bruce records. Meanwhile, what have you got? A wife who loves you, two well-adjusted children, a fine home, a good income, a respectable calling and a two thousand year old religion

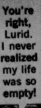

You're right, Lurid. I never realized my life was so empty!

"An electronic computer and a bikini swim suit are very much alike . . . they both eliminate a great deal of guesswork!"
—Alfred E. Neuman

LITTLE ORPHAN ANNIE

Chapter One

See the Super Patriot.
Hear him preach how he loves his country.
Hear him preach how he hates "Liberals"...
And "Moderates"... and "Intellectuals"...
And "Activists"... and "Pacifists"...
And "Minority Groups"... and "Aliens"...
And "Unions"... and "Teenagers"...
And the "Very Rich"... and the "Very Poor"...
And "People With Foreign-Sounding Names".
Now you know what a Super Patriot is.
He's someone who loves his country
While hating 93% of the people who live in it.

PLAYOY

SERENADE TO A SPORTS CAR
(Sung to the tune of "Born Free")

MG—
I live just to touch you!
When I double-clutch you,
MG, it gives me a thrill!

MG—
I love your ignition,
Your four-speed transmission,
Your points, your plugs and your grill!

MG—
When I look inside you,
The sight of each piston rod
Brings me closer to God!

MG—
I'll wash you and wax you!
If some Chevy smacks you,
I'll die, M . . . . G . . . . !

I
YOU SHALL HAVE NO OTHER GODS BESIDES ME

What in heaven's name is the use of a commandment like this? What gods are there besides him? In a day when men are questioning whether even God himself might not be dead, surely there is no doubt but that the gods are lost and gone forever—with no one being so much as dreadful sorry, Clementine. The situation may well have God beside himself, but who else is there that could be besides him? Where have all the powers gone? Aton, Marduk, Dagon, Baal? Zeus, Apollo, Diana, Neptune? Tiu, Woden, Thor, Frigga?

And then again, it is doubtful that these gods ever were for real; so, even in Moses' day, how could one "have" a god that didn't even exist?

But to talk thus about "having" a god is not so much to make a claim about something that may or may not exist out there as to say something about how I am acting in here. It is not so much a question of what gods *are* as what gods are *for*; and they are *for* to be worshiped. Whatever you worship is your god; and everyone worships, because to worship is to treat something as being the greatest ever, the center around which life revolves, the measure of one's existence, the value above every other value. Locate what it is that you act toward in this way, and you have named your god.

But, the commandment suggests, free men will take care that their worship is devoted solely to the one God Yahweh, the God of Freedom. To share his worship with any other god or god-substitute is to court enslavement, because none of them are big enough and great enough and real enough to merit or sustain one's allegiance and commitment of life. Center on something too small, and you will find yourself cutting the circle of a merry-go-round or rat race rather than orbiting the great wide universe that God made, and of which he is himself the center and axis.

Paul Fabb, on page 23, reveals the god who most often is set up beside Yahweh, and has been so since Moses' day; it is none other than Paul Fabb himself—not Fabb as Fabb, of course, but as each person wanting to be his own god. Almost every word he speaks to the interviewer points toward what we defined above as being worship. And, sad to say, all in the world **MAD** had to do was just slightly exaggerate the disease from which we all suffer. But being your own god is like trying to lift yourself by your own bootstraps; the worshiper is a heavier lump than the god can manage.

This Fabb is an evangelist, too. He is out to finagle others into worshiping his god. And some fools fall for it—such as the gal with loads of personality and absolutely no brains.

To be your own god might seem a mark of freedom; but is it? Is Fabb a free man? Hardly—although it is a little difficult to decide who is sicker, who is most enslaved to whom: Fabb the god or Fabb the worshiper.

On page 25, the Rev. Dr. Burton Hooey preaches us quite a sermon about how sweet it is to switch gods, set up one beside another, whenever an attractive one comes along. Who (or better, what) is his god?

In the last frame, he gives a neat hint regarding how to go about god-swapping without losing your pulpit; use a little mumbo-jumbo to preserve your piety and make as if the whole business was God's idea to begin with. Of course, there is a verse in the Bible that says, "God is not mocked"—but it is not that God immediately has to knock him down; much simpler, Hooey, on his own, has traded away the freedom to become a true man. Color him "slave."

The *Playboy* page presents a miscellany of "besides" gods. Things which are all to the good when treated properly destroy a person's freedom when they are worshiped as gods. With Daddy Warbucks it is the almighty dollar. With our artist-photographer (as with many others) self rates even over sex—or sex becomes nothing more than a ritual in the worship of self.

The patriotic love of country very easily can slide into worship of a "god besides." The nation may seem to be big enough and great enough and good enough to function as a god. But, as a god, the nation is as false as any other. Notice into how small a circle the Super Patriot gets trapped, loving his country while hating 93 percent of the people who make it up.

You've heard of "my mother the car"; much closer to home you may find "my god the car."

And for the worship of what god is *Playboy* the Bible? *Playboy* may promise sabbath rest for the people of god—but not in *Abraham's* bosom.

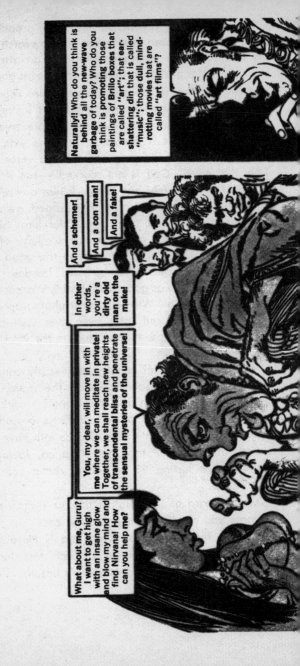

36

37

CHAPTER 1.

What is a fad?
What is a fetish?
Here is a simple explanation:
See that shop window mannequin?
She has a mini skirt,
She has green stockings,
She has large sunglasses,
And she has hanging earrings.
If a girl wears these things because "everyone is doing it,"
That is a fad.
If a fellow wears them,
That is a fetish.

HOW DO YOU LIKE MY BEARD? DOESN'T IT MAKE ME LOOK MASCULINE AND DISTINGUISHED AND ARTY AND NON-CONFORMIST? THAT'S WHY I GREW IT! YOU SEE, ACTUALLY, I'M RATHER SHY AND CLODDISH AND DULL AND SQUARE!

"Most of us don't know exactly what we want, but we're pretty sure we don't have it!"—Alfred E. Neuman

THE DYLA MONSTER
(Raucus Incomprehensibus)

The Dyla Monster is not a monster at all; he just looks that way. Actually, he is an intelligent creature with a very important message, but he is unable to communicate it normally. So the message comes across as an incoherent rasping whine. The Dyla Monster lets his hair grow wild so he won't resemble his enemies, the Fat Cats *(Squarus Conformi)*, whom he hates because of their considerable wealth, status and material possessions. Today, the Dyla Monster is an exalted creature who has managed to gather up considerable wealth, status and material possessions.

BULLETS THROUGH MY HEART

with

Vera Hruba Ralston
George Brent
Donald Crisp

and

Marsha Hunt as "Irving"

Before television, if a person wanted to be entertained, he'd have to go to the movies—which in those days were nothing more than trashy, poorly written dull melodramas.

BULLETS THROUGH MY HEART

with

Vera Hruba Ralston
George Brent
Donald Crisp

and

Marsha Hunt as "Irving"

Today, thanks to television, a person merely has to turn a knob to be entertained in the comfort of his own home.

"Everyone knows the difference
between 'right' and 'wrong'. . .
it's just that some people
can't make a decision!"
—Alfred E. Neuman

There's nothing like spending a nice, average evening at home in quiet, suburban Big Sewer, California, and inviting two plain, average suburban friends over to sculpture me in the nude.

It's amazing how just one hunk of wood can help turn a dirty scene into an artistic one!

47

II
YOU SHALL NOT MAKE FOR YOURSELF A GRAVEN IMAGE

Think about it: in the ancient world, art was done not so much for art's sake as for the sake of some god or other. Recall all you know about Egyptian and Mesopotamian art, or look at pictures in a book. Beetles (scarabs), lotuses, sphinxes, winged horses with human heads, the sun, moon, and stars—all were accompaniments of worship. And even when you see the statue of a pharaoh ten times as big as life, you can be sure that it represents an attempt to make a god out of him. Kings liked to think of themselves as pretty big stuff, but none of them were that big.

This is what art was in Moses' world; and against this background, the second commandment begins to make good sense. The original intention may have been to prohibit Israel from using images to represent Yahweh in the way that other peoples used images to represent their gods. Of course! If Yahweh is creator and lord of the whole universe, then to identify him with any part of that universe or any creature within it is to point too low. Inevitably the god of the image is bound to become too small and constricted to be Yahweh.

On the other hand, it may be that the original intention in prohibiting images was to discourage the introduction of gods besides Yahweh. Either way, this commandment is little more than a supplement to the first one. In fact, in some traditions the commandments are so numbered that this one is treated as a part of Number 1 rather than being Number 2.

However, we can extend the principle behind it just enough to suit our **MAD** purposes. "To *have* gods besides me," we said, was to take something other than God as the center and source of our lives; on the other hand, "to *make* an image" is to treat something as being considerably more valuable and important than it actually is. If, for example, you let some TV commercial convince you that the use of a certain mouthwash is the key to social acceptance, happiness, and success, what has happened? You have made for yourself an image that inflates something real small into a very big picture—and, without fail, this means that some truly great interest gets relegated to a minor slot. One becomes a slave to the very image he creates.

In our day and age, image-making has reached a height that puts the ancient world in the shade; the commandment now is more to the point than ever it has been before. Image-making is what our society does best. One of our largest and most lucrative industries—centering at Madison Avenue, New York— is devoted to image-making, pure and simple (or perhaps impure and as complicated as all get-out).

MAD's Ed Sullivan takeoff on the Wizard of Oz suggests that the whole "new wave" culture is a graven image. Do you buy that?

Betty of the Pimples makes a less obvious but perhaps more important point: Wouldn't it be better to be content simply to be who you are and work at being the best you you can possibly be, rather than to set up a stereotype image of a normal, happy, typical, fun-loving teen-ager and knock yourself out trying to fit it? Talk about slavery!

The next page lifts up a variety of graven images: the graven image of clothing fashions, the graven image of distinguished masculinity, the graven image of what passes for music—all of them insignificances blown up out of all proportion. And the neatest switch is there in the Charlie Brown Cartoon. Simply take an honest-to-goodness person like Charlie Brown and put him in the role of a big business executive; this immediately reveals how empty an image that role can be.

The following pages focus upon the entertainment media—movies, TV, stage, publishing. These industries claim to be serving the people by giving them what they want, but it can be asked whether the industries do not themselves create the images that create the wants that consequently "will bring them back much dough . . . dough . . . dough . . . dough." Rather obviously, we are all in this image-making business together; and once again Moses would throw down the tablets if he were to see us dancing around our golden calves.

The nude bits on pages 45-46 call for further comment. What would be the funniest image ever made, if it were not being worshiped so seriously, is this nudity thing. To suggest that the willingness to take off one's clothes in public is significant, important, a sign of freedom, of becoming a true person, of mankind's achieving humanity . . . Strip a person of his clothes and find—a god. If this is it, this act that requires nothing of intelligence, wisdom, art, skill, or ability but only brazen shamelessness; then behold the new man: the Neanderthal who never once let clothing hide our view of his true humanity. Thank God that Alfred E. Neuman has gotten into the act and shown up this image for the freedom it represents—that of a poor sucker who has hooked himself in the britches.

The Chant For Peace

With a P and an E and an A C E!
That's what we're after—yessiree!
Show to the world how we hate war—
Fill up the quad with blood and gore!
We've got a cause that's good and clean!
Burn down the buildings! Cream the Dean!
Build up a world that's fair and free—
Death to the pigs who don't agree!
Then, when we've smashed the fa-cul-ty—
We'll have P and an E and an A C E!

The Berkeley Cop-Rouser

You dirty ▬▬▬▬▬ *!*
You slimy ▬▬▬▬▬ *!*
▬▬ *you!* ▬▬▬ *you!*
And ▬▬▬ *you, too!*
If you don't like it,
▬▬*!* ▬▬*!* ▬▬*!* ▬▬*!*
Rah!

llowmen who respect and honor him. How can one
aim to be loving either God or his neighbor while
sing language that is disrespectful of both?

But even if God were left entirely out of the picture,
profanity is a sin against the mother tongue. Consider
that the capability of speech, or verbal communication, is one of the most precious gifts possessed by
man. To the best of our knowledge, man is the only
creature in the whole wide universe who has been
given this ability; and clearly, this ability has been
a vital factor in the status, dignity, and power that
he has been able to achieve over all other creatures
and over his physical and social environment. Speech
is one of the keys to our humanity. And it is obvious
that speech can perform its true function as a means of
humanization only if words are used in a way that
<del>value as communi-</del>

Don't You Hate . . . cretins who play brilliant phone games
like talking dirty, or asking stupid questions, or
laughing, or screaming, etc., and then hanging up!

III

YOU SHALL NOT TAKE THE NAME OF THE LORD YOUR GOD IN VAIN

Contrary to the common understanding, this commandment was not originally directed against what we call profanity. It didn't have to be. It is extremely unlikely that any early Hebrew would have used the name of God in a careless, unthinking way. He might slip back into polytheism (the worship of gods in addition to or other than Yahweh), or into idolatry (the worship of images), but even so, he would not be flip about either his god or any other. A god—any god —to him represented the sort of power and dignity that deserved respect.

Indeed, sometime after the period of the Ten Com-

mandments the Hebrews became so imp the holiness of Yahweh that they chose not name with their sinful lips—not even in w alone in vain. So completely did they avoid sp that they actually forgot how it was pronoun recovery of the original name Yahweh is a very development.

In truth, then, the illustrations on the prece pages get closer to the biblical understanding of commandment than do those seen here. However, cause profanity has become a problem in our day, is proper that we (and **MAD**) extend the command ment to make it apply.

It seems unlikely that many of the people who swear actually intend that their language be taken literally. They are not praying a solemn prayer to God desiring that he strike someone down, send them to

Don't You Hate . . . cretins who play brilliant phone games like talking dirty, or asking stupid questions, or laughing, or screaming, etc., and then hanging up!

III
YOU SHALL NOT
TAKE THE NAME
OF THE
LORD YOUR GOD IN
VAIN

Contrary to the common understanding, this commandment was not originally directed against what we call profanity. It didn't have to be. It is extremely unlikely that any early Hebrew would have used the name of God in a careless, unthinking way. He might slip back into polytheism (the worship of gods in addition to or other than Yahweh), or into idolatry (the worship of images), but even so, he would not be flip about either his god or any other. A god—any god —to him represented the sort of power and dignity that deserved respect.

Indeed, sometime after the period of the Ten Commandments the Hebrews became so impressed with the holiness of Yahweh that they chose not to speak his name with their sinful lips—not even in worship, let alone in vain. So completely did they avoid speaking it that they actually forgot how it was pronounced; the recovery of the original name Yahweh is a very recent development.

In truth, then, the illustrations on the preceding pages get closer to the biblical understanding of the commandment than do those seen here. However, because profanity has become a problem in our day, it is proper that we (and **MAD**) extend the commandment to make it apply.

It seems unlikely that many of the people who swear actually intend that their language be taken literally. They are not praying a solemn prayer to God desiring that he strike someone down, send them to hell, or damn them for eternity. If one's profanity were this, then it would be the expression of a quality of hatred and despicability that might better be considered under the commandment, "You shall not kill." Wouldn't it be weird if many of those who are protesting the napalm burning of men, women, and children in Vietnam in the process actually were praying that God burn other men endlessly in the fires of hell? **MAD** senses something of this contradiction in its "Top College Cheers."

Yet even if by far the greatest amount of profanity is not intended with full seriousness, a serious issue still is involved. To use the name of God and other God words in a flip and careless way certainly implies that the speaker does not truly believe that there is a God who hears men, or who has any concern about how they act or how they feel toward him. At the very least, profanity displays perhaps even a subconscious contempt for God and for those of one's fellowmen who respect and honor him. How can one claim to be loving either God or his neighbor while using language that is disrespectful of both?

But even if God were left entirely out of the picture, profanity is a sin against the mother tongue. Consider that the capability of speech, or verbal communication, is one of the most precious gifts possessed by man. To the best of our knowledge, man is the only creature in the whole wide universe who has been given this ability; and clearly, this ability has been a vital factor in the status, dignity, and power that he has been able to achieve over all other creatures and over his physical and social environment. Speech is one of the keys to our humanity. And it is obvious that speech can perform its true function as a means of humanization only if words are used in a way that preserves their meaning and their value as communicators of thought and reason.

If, then, the clear meaning of terms (such as the name of God) are carelessly disregarded and the words used deliberately to express, not thought, but blind, uncontrolled passion, then the gift of language is cheapened and undercut. It is a human tragedy when, as happens in the movie *Virginia Woolf* (illustrated on page 53), a college professor and his wife, people who ought to appreciate the significance of words, instead should resort to profanity as a means of bludgeoning one another, stripping one another of human dignity and self-respect. It is through speech that our free humanity comes into being. How sad that speech also should be used to reverse that process.

And how sad, too, that, as the **MAD** excerpt suggests, this movie should be the breakthrough that established lush profanity as being smart, the "in" thing that makes for box-office.

Chapter Six

See the Yippies.
They are preventing a building from being torn down.
See them lie in front of the bulldozer.
See them throw stones at the workmen.
See them hold their breath and turn blue.
Who lives in the building?
One poor, oppressed, perverted Junkie.
The Yippies are protecting the Junkie's right.
The Yippies are demonstrating their Compassion.
The Yippies are acting in the name of Humanity.
Which is why they want to save the building.
So it can't be torn down for a Hospital.

Chapter Nine

See the Rabble Rouser.
Somehow, he has become an Ordained Minister
Even though he hasn't been inside a church
In 20 years.
The Rabble Rouser delivers a weekly broadcast
Called "The Holy Crusade of Heaven".
(Or is it "The Heavenly Crusade of Holiness"?)
The broadcast accomplishes two things:
It gives him a platform
For spewing Hatred and Bigotry.
And it gives him a Tax-Free income
As head of a "Religious Organization".
Why is the Rabble Rouser allowed on the Air?
God only knows!

Chapter 5.

See the Funeral Orator.
He has an important mission.
It is his job
To make the mourners who feel bad
Feel worse.
He says such nice things about the Dear Departed.
Isn't it a shame that he never *knew* the Dear Departed?
Funeral Orators always say such nice things at funerals.
It makes you begin to feel that only nice people die.
Doesn't that raise a theological question in your mind?
Listen to the Funeral Orator say,
"He was a wonderful man."
"He was a devoted Husband and Father."
See the mourners.
See their shocked faces.
No wonder they are shocked.
The Dear Departed
Was a Woman!

"SHPIEL"

But the worst contamination of all will come from the publicity-seeking Politicians who continue to belch forth into our atmosphere outraged statements, dull harangues and empty campaign promises to solve our nation's problems—and all calculated to gain support and votes.

And do you know what I promise to do about the problem of Air Pollution! I promise to go down to Washington . . . and shut my mouth!

"There's one thing we know for sure about the speed of light. It gets here too early in the morning!"—Alfred E. Neuman

Yahweh...

The third commandment did not prohibit profanity; there was no profanity around to prohibit. What it had in mind as taking Yahweh's name "in vain" was magic, the use of incantations, charms, curses, and all such truck.

In the ancient world, it was widely believed that to know a person's name (whether the name of a human person or a god person) gave one a certain power over him. If the name were used in a magic formula, then the speaking of that name could make things happen to the person, or could force him to perform certain actions. The name of a god was particularly powerful, of course, because through the proper sort of prayers and incantations one could make the god act favorably toward oneself and unfavorably toward one's enemies.

Indeed, it may well be that a good example comes in the third chapter of Exodus, where God first meets Moses at the burning bush and commissions him to go down to Egypt land and tell old pharaoh. Some scholars believe that Moses is so insistent about knowing God's name precisely because he intends to use it for magical purposes. And it may be that when God explains that the name "Yahweh" means "I am who I am," he is saying in effect: "I am not going to give

64

you any such names, Moses. I don't intend to be manipulated by you or anyone else. I am who I am. I will come and go as I choose. I will do as it seems to me wise to do. Don't try to use your magic to make this God do tricks for you because it just won't work." Even before the third commandment got commanded, God had taken steps to prevent his name from being taken in vain—by coming forth as the God without a name.

And now for a shocker: the place where the third commandment most often gets broken, where the Lord's name is taken most in vain, is probably in *church*. Seriously, whenever men, instead of sincerely seeking to find *God's* will for *their* lives, try to follow *their own* will or impose it on others by using God's name so as to make it appear that it is *his* will they want done—this, in the original sense of the third commandment, is to take the name of the Lord your God in vain. And consciously or unconsciously, a great deal of this does go on in the church.

Some of the church's most central rituals usually are performed in such a way as definitely to suggest that when men go through the proper motions and speak the proper words, God *has* to act toward them in a certain way.

Other examples are more to the point of the **MAD**ness on the preceding pages. The Yippies, of course, do not act in the name of the biblical God; humanity is the god they name. But, truth to tell, they often manage to take even the name of humanity in vain, to act in the name of humanity in a way which amounts to a betrayal of humanity. And the Yippies are not the only ones who do this, either.

The air-polluting "shpiel" of the politician (commemorated on page 63) is another instance of man's growth into humanity being repressed in the name in the name of humanity. In this regard, one of **MAD's** strengths is its beautiful "a plague on both your houses" approach—as, in this instance, both the Yippies and their most vocal opponents, yammer-mouthed politicians, are shown to be guilty of breaking the same commandment.

The illustration on page 60 is a well-aimed hit. It is true that Christian missionary work often has been an instrument for imposing Western culture upon non-Western peoples. Now the original Christianity of the New Testament was as much or more Eastern than Western and freely adaptable to any and all cultures. But we were not content with original Christianity, and so oftentimes have forced upon innocent people a version that smacks as much or more of "Westernism" than of Christianity. And to the extent that we have preached our own folkways as being the will *of God,* to that extent we have taken the Lord's name in vain.

The Rabble Rouser and the Funeral Orator are two self-evident examples (that is, self-evident once **MAD** has made them so) of how the name of God can be used to promote ungodly ends. You probably can add other specimens to this catalog. But let us be grateful that **MAD** is as brave to let fly at the church as at any other institution of society. The church needs to be reminded of the Ten Commandments too.

America, the Beautiful - Revisited

Oh, beautiful...

CONCEPT:
FRANK JACOBS

PRODUCED BY:
MAX BRANDEL

PICTURES BY:
U.P.I. & W.W.

for spacious skies...

for amber waves of grain...

for purple mountain majesties...

above the fruited plain...

America, America...

God shed His grace on thee...

and crown thy good with brotherhood...

from sea to shining sea.

SUPERMAN

72

EXPLORING
UNDERWATER

The waters around us, whether ocean or lake, abound with magnificent marine life. The Diver will be richly rewarded if he is alert and observant and seeks them out.

Here is a lovely sight to see—a bayscallop skipping gaily through placid water.

Snails are plentiful, and they are fun to watch as they slowly wend their way.

74

Bright colored underwater plants sway to and fro like graceful ballet dancers.

Many varieties of fish will float lazily by in swiftly moving currents and eddies.

'Golf and Success are very similar: you strive to get to the green . . and then you're in the hole!''—Alfred E. Neuman

The greatest thing to happen to Pro Football, of course, was the concept of **"The Super Bowl"** on **"Super Sunday"**. . . and all of the "Super" things that came with it. In a moment, we'll meet one of the men responsible for the **effective promotion** of "Super Sunday". . . but first, I'd like to show you this last slide depicting a typical American town last January:

The Sunday Drivers' Cheer
(to the tune of "On Wisconsin")

On you drivers!
On you drivers!
Inch your way along!
Heading for a Sunday outing—
Fifty million strong (*Stop honking!*)

See them lined up—
We will wind up
Home at 10 o'clock!
And to think we only drove
A-round the block!

IV

REMEMBER THE SABBATH DAY, TO KEEP IT HOLY

Where the Hebrew practice of a weekly sabbath came from and just what it originally signified is a problem that Old Testament scholars have found virtually unsolvable. They can trace elements both of a taboo day (negative) and a festival day (positive). Let us look first at the festival aspect which clearly dominates the commandment in its present form. Some scholars believe that a taboo form which would parallel most of the other commandments (namely, "You shall not work on the sabbath") was original but that this was changed precisely so that the festival aspect could dominate.

One day a week was set aside for religious observances in honor of Yahweh, and this was understood as being a *festival*—nothing more nor less than a *fun* day. Just how the ancient Hebrews went about en-joying Yahweh we don't know; but it is obvious that in our day we have the matter twisted wrong way around. We want a fun day all right, but we think that the way to have fun is by forgetting God rather than remembering him. **MAD** tells the truth of the matter on the preceding pages.

Perhaps part of the fault is the church's in not showing us how the worship of God can be fun. But more of the fault is ours in not having gotten to know God well enough to discover that he is fun to be with. The ancient Hebrews and some moderns know; most people do not. A weekly Yahweh party can be of more real thrill and satisfaction than all our frantic efforts to enjoy-enjoy without him.

But the important point is that, far from wanting to impose some sort of morbid religious duty upon man, the fourth commandment is an invitation to the festival of God. It is one day a week in which man can be truly free and become even freer by associat-ing in a special way with the God of freedom.

Recall what was said earlier about how *negative* commands can be a door to freedom, and the sabbath as a *taboo* day opens an entirely new line of thought. The cue is the biblical statement that enlarges upon the commandment: "[On the sabbath] you shall not do any work. . . . For in six days Yahweh made heaven and earth, the sea, and all that is in them, and rested the seventh day."

The implication here is very strong that the creation itself is so put together that it carries built-in rhythms that define its most effective operation. Just as the timing must be right for an engine to run, so are there timings which must be observed if man and the uni-verse are going to run as they ought.

The fundamental alternation that God has built into things and now would teach to man, the commandment states, is that between labor and rest. Six days work and one day rest—and even the cattle need and deserve it, the scripture notes. And we might note, although the scripture does not, that too much rest and too little labor will throw the rhythm out of whack just as surely as too much labor and too little rest will.

"Do you want to be a free man and stay that way?" Yahweh asks. "Then remember the rhythms upon which the universe is constructed and keep them holy."

But there are involved many more rhythms than just the one of labor and rest. It would seem entirely proper to extend the commandment to cover them as well. The preceding pages from **MAD** can help us do just that.

The feature "America, the Beautiful—*Revisited*" is worth a year's subscription. Nine eloquent photographs speak volumes about how we have wasted and destroyed the God-given beauty of America— simply because we have broken the fourth commandment and failed to remember and keep holy the balances and rhythms upon which the life of men and the world are based.

Some of these balances, notice, concern our social life, the life of men together. Others concern the life of our natural environment. But notice, too, how these get intertwined with one another. To lose the rhythm at one point soon throws off the timing of the whole.

"Remember the sabbath day, to keep it holy" is not simply a "religious" commandment, because, in the sense it understands, the very universe itself is religious and is to be treated as holy.

...When It Comes To
"Father-Son Relationship"

Steve Cowznofski's Dad was always too busy for him. When the Old Man wasn't working, he'd never pay attention to Steve. He'd have fun with his cronies.

Since his childhood rejection left such scars on his psyche, Steve decided never to be too busy for his kids. He just didn't reckon on the possibility that they might be too busy for him. And after all, what kind of a welcome can a Father really expect when he comes home from the office empty-handed?

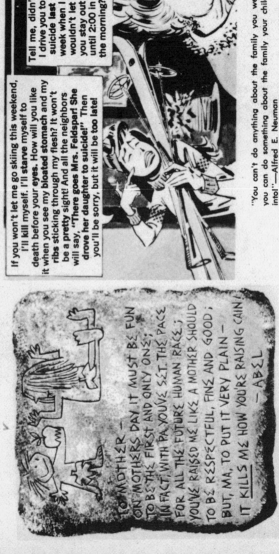

"You can't do anything about the family you were born into, but you can do something about the family your children will be born into!"—Alfred E. Neuman

V
HONOR
YOUR FATHER
AND
YOUR MOTHER

This is the one! Designed especially for parents to quote at their teen-agers! A God-given club with which to beat one's kids into submission! Right?

Wrong! It won't wash. In the original setting among the early Hebrews, to what audience would the Ten Commandments have been particularly addressed, do you think? To the adults, most assuredly, and even more specifically to the men, the heads of houses. According to the family structure of that day, these fathers would then have the responsibility of passing on, interpreting, and seeing through the operation of the commandments in the lives of their families.

It does not make sense, then, that right in the middle of instructions to the family heads there should be one commandment directed to an entirely different audience. But there is another aspect of the Hebrew family structure that we are likely to overlook. The Hebrew family unit inevitably must have included elderly people, grandparents, the fathers and mothers of the family heads themselves. In its original intent, then, the commandment probably said in effect, "Men, when your aged parents get to the place that they no longer are productive, no longer paying their way, this is no grounds for turning them out or ceasing to care for them. Honor your father and mother."

Some scholars believe that this commandment originally may have agreed with the others in being worded in the negative: You shall not curse . . . , or perhaps more likely, You shall not *despise* your father and mother. The change was made in order to stress that one's obligation to his parents goes beyond simply avoiding a negative attitude toward them and enjoins the truly positive attitude of honor and respect.

Yet, having said all this, it is obvious that the extension of the commandment to cover the attitude of children and teen-agers toward their parents is a legitimate one. In fact, we intend to run the extension even further and make the commandment read: Honor not only *your* father and mother but anyone else's father and mother, anyone who might at some time become a father or mother, and the children of all fathers and mothers. Did we miss anybody?

The Ten Commandments certainly did not mean to limit such widespread honoring; and at other points in the Bible the implication is made explicit (whether you prefer the negative or the positive wording): "See that you do not despise one of these little ones" (Matthew 18:10). "Honor all men" (1 Peter 2:17).

So, although it is entirely out of order for parents to preach this commandment at their children as though it applied only to the children and not to themselves as well, nevertheless it is in place for us and

MAD to consider the ways in which young people honor or fail to honor their parents.

MAD has hit it about right, hasn't it, when it hints that we often take our parents for granted, treat them as though they exist only for our own benefit and convenience rather than as people who have some needs, desires, and rights of their own?

And is there not in all of us at least something of a Vicki Feldspar who does her durndest to wheedle, inveigle, and manipulate her parents into letting her have her own way? How often do we make our parents out as being "ruthless, cruel, dictatorial, oppressive, and domineering" when down deep we know that they truly are interested in our welfare and, more often than not, actually do ask of us only what is good for us?

Honoring one's father and mother is not such an exorbitant demand. It does not mean that one is to worship them (the first commandment outlaws that). It means simply to treat them as persons, showing them the same honesty, appreciation, love, and respect that you want them to show you.

CHAPTER 5.

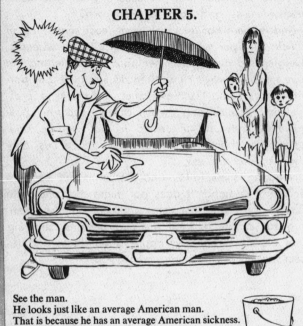

See the man.
He looks just like an average American man.
That is because he has an average American sickness.
He has a car fetish.
He washes his car.
He waxes his car.
He polishes his car.
He treats his car better than he treats his family.
Does that mean he does not love his family?
No, it only means
He is more emotionally involved with his car.

CHAPTER 6.

See the teenage girl?
She has a "doll fetish".
At her age, too.
She goes to bed with a stuffed Panda,
A plush Lion and a cuddly French Poodle.
Does she go to bed with just any doll?
No, she is not that kind of girl.
Poor kid. Someday she will realize
That is useless to love an unfeeling object.
Unfeeling objects cannot love her in return.
She already realizes this
About her parents.

"Efficiency Experts are smart enough to tell you how to run your business, and too smart to start one of their own!"—Alfred E. Neuman

Chapter 8.

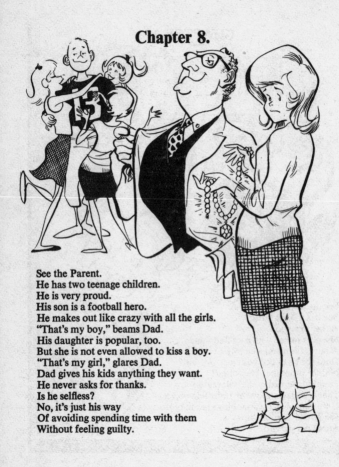

See the Parent.
He has two teenage children.
He is very proud.
His son is a football hero.
He makes out like crazy with all the girls.
"That's my boy," beams Dad.
His daughter is popular, too.
But she is not even allowed to kiss a boy.
"That's my girl," glares Dad.
Dad gives his kids anything they want.
He never asks for thanks.
Is he selfless?
No, it's just his way
Of avoiding spending time with them
Without feeling guilty.

Mr. Leech, can you explain why toys that are worth only 20¢ or 30¢ sell so well at $5.00 or $10.00?

You have to understand the psychology of toy buyers. Now, who buys the most toys?

Parents, I guess.

Right. And since most parents hate to **spend** time with their kids, they **feel guilty.** So they spend **money** on them instead. Now, if a father were to buy a toy and spend only **30¢,** it would **still** leave him with a lot of **guilt** feelings left over. If he spent **$10** for the **same** toy, he'd not only feel **content,** but he'd **also** figure he's entitled to **appreciation.**

The beautiful thing about **MAD** (in spite of all its uglies) is that it has eyes enough to see both ways. "Children, honor your parents"? Yes; but also, "Parents, honor your children!" The one case is no less demanded than the other.

Of course, *the way in which* parents honor children will show up as somewhat different from *the way in which* children honor parents; but both are to be true and appropriate expressions of honor. The commandment does not suggest that everyone is to be treated as though they were children—nor as though all were parents. The secret is to find the sort of honor that is suitable to the age and situation of the people involved and the nature of their relationship.

A wise columnist has suggested that one reason why our society at present is having so much trouble with the generation gap is because we have not let it be as wide as it should be. Too many adults are trying to play it as though they were still teen-agers, and too many teen-agers are trying to play it as though they already were mature adults. And when the actors all are trying to read the lines of everyone else's script, it is no wonder that the play gets fouled up. A child cannot honor his parents while refusing to accept the offspring role, and a father or mother cannot honor his children while evading the parent role.

This commandment, as the others, has to do with freedom. Children can be free in their relationship to their parents and parents can be free in relationship to their children only as each accepts his own role and honors the other party in his.

On the pages before us, **MAD** illustrates some of the ways in which parents fail to be true parents and so lose the possibility of truly honoring their children.

The interesting thing to note is that parental failure to honor children springs from the same defect as children's failure to honor their parents. In either case, there is a self-centeredness that basically does not want to be bothered with the other person, an attitude that puts one's own concerns, interests, and pleasures above his desire to be open and helpful toward the other person.

It is noteworthy that the word "love" is not so much as mentioned in the Ten Commandments (except in the addendum to the one concerning graven images and then not in connection with the man-to-man relationship). However, the word "honor" may be even more basic than "love," for honor defines the core of what true love is. Perhaps, then, this commandment is just what the present *love* generation needs; the honoring of one another would put some guts into all the love-love-loving that has tended to become so shallow and meaningless.

K K K

This extremely difficult-to-swallow cross-shaped pill seems to arrest mental development and induce pyromania, transvestism, and a red neck. Users are particularly sensitive to color, and have strong aversions to all foreign objects. Devotees like to congregate in Southern swamps before taking their mind-blowing "trips".

I is for Integration
Which millions are for
(Just so long as it doesn't
Take place right next door)!

Oh, nothing can stop us!

We'll all be free!
We'll segregate!
We'll have white slaves!!

Oh, we'll have plenty of justice,
Yes, justice is what we all crave.
We'll . . . have our land,
We'll help our folks
From the cradle until
The grave.

97

I suppose the fact that you are of one color and he another is in most instances evidence enough that he is not your father or mother, but according to our reading of the commandment he is to be honored just the same. In fact, the place where our poor old world is most loudly crying for people to do a little honoring is across lines of color, creed, and race.

More crucial than integration, equal opportunity, job training, poverty programs, or any such things is the simple honoring of one another. If that comes, these other things can be managed with no sweat; until such honoring does come, none of these other programs will make much headway. As the Kerner Report concluded, the problem is racism; and racism is nothing more nor less than some people despising other people and failing to honor them.

Again, the command to honor asks no very great big thing of us. We are not asked to act as though any person of another race were just the greatest ever to have come down the pike; race itself can become a god besides Yahweh, whether the person worships his own race or some other. All the commandment asks is that we credit the honest truth that this man of another color is a human being (just as I am) who needs and expects to receive the very same things I need and expect to receive, namely, the opportunity and wherewithal to become the truest human being I am capable of becoming. This much we owe to one another, and to recognize this debt is what it means to honor the other.

Our pages from **MAD** are arranged deliberately—another example of the insistence that the slash cut both ways. On pages 95 and 97 white racism gets the shaft; on page 96 it is black racism. Either, both, any, and all varieties of racism are equally violations of the fifth commandment.

This is one characteristic that all scholarship has noted about the Ten Commandments. Most legal codes consist of what is called "conditional law," that is, the command is hedged about with all sorts of conditions. For example, "White people shall honor blacks; *but,* because the black people have been despised by white people for so long, they shall not be required to do this sort of honoring in their turn." In contrast, the Ten Commandments take the form of what scholars call "apodictic law," that is, it is stated flat out with no ands, ifs, buts, or maybes.

The fifth commandment doesn't care whether you are white, black, yellow, or green. It doesn't care whether, in the past, people have honored, despised, or ignored you. If you consider yourself a human being, it says, then start honoring all other persons as human beings—even if they happen to be blue with chartreuse polka dots. It's real hard to wiggle out from under the Ten Commandments—and they were built that way on purpose.

The only situation in which men ever will be free is in honoring one another; and the only way that freedom will ever come is not by demanding that others honor us, but by our taking the initiative in honoring them.

WINDOW SHOUTING

Six or eight guys pile in a car and go cruising down the main street. The one sitting in the front on the right (who is usually the best "make-out") becomes the "Window Man." He leans out as they pass females, and shouts clever, daring pick-up phrases like "Say, aren't you Doc Finster's daughter?," "Wanna lift?," "Hubba-hubba!" and "Man, I go ape over freckles!" Then they go and shout these same clever phrases at women **under** 40!

**WHEN THE HOSTESS ASKS
A LEADING QUESTION LIKE:**

**THE INCONSIDERATE GUEST
REPLIES RUDELY LIKE THIS:**

**BUT THE CONSIDERATE GUEST
SIDESTEPS THE QUESTION:**

THE ROAD HOG

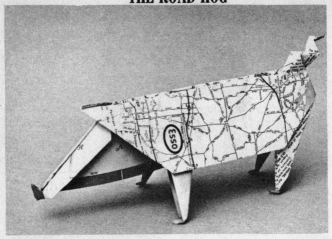

Don't You Hate . . . talkative barbers with bad breath!

This matter of honoring one another is a real tricky one because sometimes, in our zeal to get Mr. White to honor Mr. Black (or Mr. America to honor Mr. Vietnam), in the process we cease to honor Mr. White and Mr. America. In the effort to get others to obey the fifth commandment we break it ourselves.

One basic (but too seldom considered) way in

which we honor one another is through what are called the "common courtesies." In our day, however, there are signs that they are becoming more and more uncommon. **MAD** sees this and devotes considerable space to exposing the discourtesy that marks modern society.

It is something strange that the generation which has shown the most concern that the blacks, the poor, and the disadvantaged of the world be honored (and thank God for this concern) is at the same time the generation that has shown perhaps the least concern in honoring the people met in everyday contact. The popular vocabulary that makes a big word out of "brother" (black brother or Vietnamese brother) makes an equally big word out of "pig." Alongside the big word "love" stands the big obscenity "F - - - you!"

The fifth commandment can help us correct this discrepancy. Its apodictic requirement, "Honor all men," denies us the luxury of deciding whom we will honor and whom despise. And perhaps it can lead us to be somewhat more thoughtful, considerate, and courteous in all our dealings with other people.

Granted, many of the expected social amenities seem to be rather trivial and insignificant customs. Nevertheless, they constitute a sign language that society has invented for itself by which one person can let another know that he honors and values him. Deliberately to reject, defy, and despise that language inevitably is to communicate that one despises the people who use it—no matter how many love placards, symbols, and insignias one might display in the meantime.

If free people are, of necessity, those who also honor one another, then free people, by the same token, also will be courteous people.

Look at the hawk.
It's a hawk that can talk.
Would you like to be talked to
by a hawk?

Who is he?
He's General Cole.
He has a dream,
he has a goal,
to solve a problem
that tries Man's soul.

Here is the plan
of General Cole:
He wants to blow
a great big hole
into the Earth
from Pole to Pole.
It's the Army's answer
to Birth Control.

THE WAR-MONGER'S ANTHEM

(Sung to the tune of "More")

War—
Helps to keep the pop-u-la-tion down!
War—
Means less people in a crowded town!
War—
Lets us try out new ar-till-er-y!
War—
Gives our soldiers foreign trips for free!

War—
Gives us heroes who are strong and good!
War—
Gives us John Wayne films from Hollywood!
War—
Gives our TV newscasts more
Scenes of blood and death and gore!
That's what Living Color's for!

War—
Helps the U.S.O.!
Yes, war—
Brings a Bob Hope show!
Yes, war—
Brings us much enjoyment
And it cuts down unemployment!

W is for World War III —
We hope we survive,
So we can prepare for
World Wars IV and V!

VI
YOU
SHALL
NOT
KILL

This commandment we intend to extend for a fare-thee-well; most people already have started the process, all unaware.

Originally this commandment was not understood as a blanket prohibition of killing. The biblical record makes it abundantly clear that the people who first received the commandment did not interpret it as outlawing either war or capital punishment. Indeed, the commandment itself makes some effort to keep from being read as a blanket prohibition. The Hebrew word for kill that appears here is not the one that normally would be expected; it seems to be a technical term of more limited application. The best suggestion scholars can come up with is that the word refers to killing which is disapproved by the community and is seen as damaging to the community. The specific reference, then, would seem to be to the practice of blood-vengeance.

The primitive custom was that if anyone deeply wronged me, I or my surviving kinsmen had the right to do him in. The commandment, then, put a check on this practice and required that capital punishment be administered only through the due process of the community. Thus the commandment marked a big advance over what had prevailed earlier, but does not speak with any great relevance to our day. At least this one commandment out of the ten has pretty well accomplished its goal: blood-vengeance killings are under fairly good control in our society.

Yet although it may not be accurate to quote this commandment in support of the points we are about to make, a look at the Bible as a whole makes it evident that the commandment eventually did get extended to cover our concerns. And it seems completely right that later men of God should have been granted an even deeper insight into the commandments than the original recipients possessed.

It must be perfectly obvious that God's will for humanity is not that people go around killing one another; indeed, it hardly takes God to point out the stupidity and lack of freedom involved in this one. And that such killing is practiced on gigantic scale, condoned and sponsored by society at large, using millions of professionals who are financed and trained solely for the purpose of killing their fellowmen—this is just plain incredible. How a race that acts this way can claim to be human is beyond me. And to claim that men, so acting, are bearers of the image of God is a libel against God.

Of course, we all know that it isn't *our* fault that

115

1969
OFFENSIVE STARS
TO WATCH

DUSTIN WILTFANG

Riot Leader Northwestern

Wiltfang earned fame when he painted himself blue during a "Filth-In" at Northwestern last year protesting U.S. Policy in South Dakota. A founder of LOVE (League to Obliterate the Vile Establishment), he forced the faculty to set up three new graduate schools . . . one for Eskimos, and two for minority groups yet to be discovered. After graduation, Wiltfang hopes to join the Viet Cong and turn "Pro."

STACY "ZAP" FLIT

Martyr
New York University

Flit's body still bears wheel marks sustained last year when he lay down in front of a baby carriage to protest "Legitimacy." Named "The Rioter of the Year" by **Ramparts** for chaining himself to the Dean of Women, he won freedom after promising amnesty to faculty members. A devout atheist, Flit believes students should never resort to peaceful negotiations until all avenues of violence have been explored.

117

ZEB ESTERHAZY

Instigator
Columbia

Six-foot-one, 170 pounds, lean, and obscene, Esterhazy ranks as one of the most deceptive Riot Instigators in the country today. During last year's "March on John Wayne," Esterhazy out-psyched Campus Police by shouting all the four-letter words known to Man in Sanskrit. A "Creative Graffiti" Major (with his Minor in "Men's Room Art"), Zeb has sworn not to take a bath until The Bronx recognizes Red China.

1969
DEFENSIVE STARS
TO WATCH

**ALGERNON
"BILLY" CLUBB**

**Head Crusher
California State Militia**

Clubb holds the 1968 NCAA (National College-Agitator Arresters) record for the number of skulls smashed on a Thursday in October. Last season, he squelched a San Francisco State "Bleed-In" with his bare hands while winning an "On-The-Field Promotion" from Corporal to Sadist. Serious and thoughtful off the field, Billy is studying nights to be a Psychopath.

CAL CUTTER

**Pummeler
Virginia State Police**

Cutter won national acclaim last season when he locked 89 rampaging Howard University students in a broom closet for three whole days. The tragic event is now referred to as "The Black Hole of Cal Cutter." When not playing Defensive Pummeler for Virginia State Police, Cal keeps his weight down to a trim 275 lbs. by organizing and training crazed lynch mobs.

HERSHEY WESTMORELAND

Sharpshooter
Michigan National Guard

In his rookie year last season, Westmoreland suffered from an over-eagerness to look good. Charged by a line of Michigan State rioters, Hershey fired a salvo over their heads, and wounded himself in the left ear. Nevertheless he stood his ground heroically, clubbing everything that moved with his riot gun, and prevented a student take-over of Lake Huron.

The March Of The Hell-Raisers
(to the tune of "Stout Hearted Men")

Give me some guys
Who are hell-raising guys
Who can shake up and break up a class!
Guys who don't care,
Who will stand on their chair,
Who will shout and give out with the sass! Yeah!

Running and romping
And screaming and stomping,
We brawl like it's all just a gas!
When—
The teacher fin'lly sees
That we don't give a hoot!

Then—
We'll start again!
Because she's just a substitute!

CHAPTER 9.
The Hockey Fan

See the typical Hockey Fan.
He loves Body Checks.
He loves to see Defensemen get kicked in the groin.
He loves to scream, "Kill the Goalie!"
Kill! Kill! Kill!
Tomorrow, he may demonstrate
Against Police Brutality in Harlem
And against the use of Napalm in Vietnam.
He considers violence to be "Un-American".
Lucky for him, most Hockey Players are Canadian.

To H. Rap Brown

You walk along a city street
    That's filled with peace and quiet;
Before you're through, you've helped to start
    A full-scale bloody riot;
You leave a trail of burned-out homes,
    Of people forming breadlines;
But what the hell! Why should you care
    So long as you get headlines!

GUNS GUNS GUNS!

BIG GUN BARGAINS

AUTHENTIC DELUXE ELEPHANT GUN

ONLY $7

FINE'S SPORTING GOODS
330 West Slaughter Street, Bangor, Maine

ALSO THESE SENSATIONAL SPECIALS!

He is busy searching for obscene mail.
Search, search, search.
He wants to make sure that sick people
Who order lethal weapons by mail
Have clean minds.

LESSON NINE

See the typical magazine ad.
See how easy it is to buy guns by mail.
Isn't it fun to buy lethal weapons by mail?
Where is your friendly Postmaster?

"Usually, when money grows on trees, there's a lot of grafting going on!"—Alfred E. Neuman

there are wars; it's all those *bad* people from other countries. And so we *have* to fight, *have* to have wars, or God's will for mankind would be permanently stymied. If we didn't fight, the world would go to hell. "Create hell in order to avert hell" is our motto.

But this line of thought has to assume that God is incapable of taking care of the race he created, that his methods won't do the job, since we feel that we have to resort to methods of our own. Surely no one would maintain that war is God's invention and not wholly our own.

But a God who is capable of raising a people out of Egyptian slavery, a Judaism out of the Babylonian holocaust, and a Christian church out of the despair of the crucifixion—he is capable of caring for any person, any nation, or any race that is willing to act truly human rather than like savage animals.

It would be foolish, of course, to claim that **MAD** supports all that we have just said, but the preceding pages do constitute evidence that it senses the problem and at least looks in our direction.

We will need to stretch this commandment just a little more in order to make it say everything we have in mind—although we are not doing anything that the Bible has not already done.

Let us translate "You shall not kill" by using a synonym that makes it read "You shall not *take life*." The difference is that kill means to make completely dead, and "take life" can be construed to cover any action that disables a person from enjoying the fullest life of which he is capable. A person can be deprived of a great deal of life before he is killed dead.

The commandment says only that "you shall not kill," but God's overarching desire is that men have *life*. The book of Deuteronomy reports a sermon that accompanies the commandments in which Moses says,

"See, I have set before you this day life and good, death and evil; . . . therefore choose life, that you and your descendants may live."

With this move we have brought under the umbrella of the sixth commandment the activity pictured on the preceding pages. Beating on people may not always be an attempt to kill them dead, but it certainly does restrict their enjoyment of life. Violence against persons is simply a less than total killing; and it can be argued that even the willful destruction of a man's property is to some degree a deprivation of his right to life.

MAD is quite aware of the violence that infects our society and frequently comments upon it. The "Eva and Dolf" satire of the movie *Bonnie and Clyde* is an outstanding example. In some countries of the world, American movies are censored more for their violence than for their explicit sex. Surely it marks some sort of perversion when people are entertained by the sight of other people being cut down, chomped up, knocked around, plowed under, and tromped over. Rome, before it fell, had its infamous gladiatorial shows. The U.S.A. (before it fell[?]) had developed a film and electronic technology that enabled people to be closer and more intimately involved as spectators of blood and gore than any Roman in the Colosseum ever could have been.

127

Of course, it is no fun simply to watch violence if one has no opportunity to practice a little on his own. So we get in our licks. The lineup of Offensive and Defensive Stars points out a current aspect of this violence—and is careful to look both ways. The implication that student versus police violence comes to about six of the one and half a dozen of the other is probably very near to being dead accurate. After all, both the students and the police are products of the same gore-glorying culture.

Pages 122-125 are a miscellany calling our attention to some outbreaks of the violence disease that we might otherwise overlook. Schoolroom hell-raising might seem to indicate a rather mild case, but the taxpayers who have to stand the cost of the malicious destruction that goes on in school buildings and other public places tend to see things a bit differently. How often have the rampages of fun-loving school kids had the effect of defeating a bond issue that would have financed better educational facilities?

The item featuring the hockey fan provokes just one simple (or perhaps not so simple) question: To what extent does the enjoyment in watching contact sports come from the perverted pleasure of viewing violence? How do you answer?

The Rap Brown valentine raises a question of its own: How far are race riots motivated by a concern for equity and justice and how far by the unholy impulse against which the sixth commandment strives to protect us? When even clergymen get in the act by vilely calling for violence for the sake of the kingdom of God, one wonders how far the sickness can go.

Several times **MAD** has commented upon the matter of gun control. There would seem to be no question but that the easy availability of guns aggravates our problem of civil violence and makes it that much more destructive. And the fact that there has appeared such deep and widespread resistance to all gun control proposals does not speak well of our willingness to curb this violence. We take back what we said earlier about the sixth commandment having been successful in eliminating the practice of blood-vengeance.

BERNIE SMOKESTACK

Fumbling for cigarettes, lighter, ash tray and the address of a chest X-ray clinic can make smoking while driving a hazard to other drivers. Especially when falling ashes start fires—like the one burning there in Bernie's lap.

MARVIN CATNAPPER

Marvin's one big problem is: he can't sleep in bed. He's up all night with insomnia. But the minute he's behind the wheel of a car, driving, he pops right off. And so do the people that he hits while he's dozing and driving.

WESLEY WRONGSIGNAL

The directional signal is often used improperly. Many drivers signal for a left turn . . . then make a right absentmindedly. Others, like Wesley here, do it because they really don't know their left from their right and vice versa.

IRVING HEADTURNER

Irving's the type of driver who constantly turns his head to the rear in order to ogle girls or talk. This drives passengers crazy . . . not because it's unsafe, but because Irving has bad breath. But even with pleasant breath, a driver who looks everywhere but frontward can be nerve-wracking . . . not to mention car, pole and fence-wracking.

DARRYL DRUNKENSLOB

Drunks like Darryl are in a class by themselves when it comes to causing property damage, injury and death. Then, there's the trouble they cause driving *cars!* But no matter how often they're warned, they'll go right out and do it again . . . acting as if they don't know what's going on . . . acting as if . . . as if they were drunk or something!

PERCY DISTRACTED

This poor schnook is often beset by a nagging wife and screaming kids. The splitting headache that he gets makes for dangerous driving . . . not because he's liable to crash accidentally, but because he'd like to do it on purpose.

HENRY ONEARM

Henry just can't resist putting an arm around any chick that rides in his car. This is especially dangerous when the chick insists upon sitting in the back seat. And the steamed-up windows don't add to safe driving conditions, either.

ZELDA BUMPERTHUMPER

No matter how much space she has, our Zelda always raps the car in front and back while parking. This in itself is not dangerous . . . but it will be later on, when the drivers of those cars in front and back try using their lights.

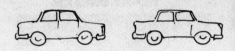

Speaking of gun control, a weapon that is much more destructive of life in our society is the automobile. Cars kill more people than guns do—including the guns and bombs of war.

To make this observation is not to suggest that cars are no different from guns and bombs. For one thing, guns and bombs represent *intentional* killing whereas car deaths are *accidental;* that is an important distinction. For another, automobiles are absolutely essential to the life of society as it is presently organized, whereas we could get along very well with many less guns, bombs, and such devices. The problem in the case of cars, then, is to use them in such a way as to minimize their destructiveness.

One approach is to build automobiles, highways, and traffic paraphernalia so that things can operate as safely as possible. The engineers, the manufacturers, and the governmental agencies that set the safety standards continually need to work this angle for all it is worth.

And in this regard, it must never be forgotten that one way in which automobiles kill (and prevent the full enjoyment of life) is by creating smog. A truly safe car must also be a smogless car; and we dare not rest until one is built.

You Shall Not Kill

However, **MAD** has it completely right: the most dangerous part of a car is the nut that holds the wheel—too often with just one hand. "You shall not kill" can accurately be translated "You shall not drive carelessly." (You didn't know that the Ten Commandments mentioned automobiles, did you?) Whoever handles a car as though it were anything but a dangerous weapon is breaking the sixth commandment (or at least bending it to where it can become broken at any moment).

The **MAD** feature points up a number of commandment benders. The list could be extended almost indefinitely; and the most serious item, speeding, does not get mentioned. But **MAD** doesn't have to tell you everything; you are smart enough to figure out some things for yourself.

Darryl Drunkenslob calls for particular comment. Liquor is involved in some 50 percent of traffic fatalities. A few more pages down the line we are going to give attention to alcohol as a killer in its own right, but here already is one big strike against it. According to commandment math, killer liquor in the driver of a killer car increases killing power in geometric rather than simply arithmetical progression. Or, for those who are not mathematically inclined: "Only a fink would drive and drink!"

We need to make one final pull in stretching the sixth commandment. A reading that must be included is "You shall not kill *yourself*," or "You shall not deprive yourself of the fullest life of which you are capable." Certainly your own life is part of the general life that God has created and which he desires for every man. But more, to the extent that you squander your own life, to that extent you also deprive your fellows of the love and service you could have devoted

"UPTIGHT" IS A DRY SUGAR CUBE

by Abu Schulz

"Uptight" means, like, a bad scene. It's when you're hung up, or wigged out, or you can't make it. We all get "uptight" once in a while. Here are some grooving examples of "uptight":

UPTIGHT is...

...seeing lilies-of-the-valley sprout
from the Marijuana seeds you planted.

UPTIGHT is...

...having the light go out on the
"joint" ... just as it gets to you.

UPTIGHT is...

...walking along the Berkeley campus
and bumping into Gov. Ronald Reagan.

UPTIGHT is...

... discovering that the flower you've been carrying in your hand for two months is actually poison sumac.

UPTIGHT is...

... taking an LSD trip and seeing "The Mormon Tabernacle Choir".

UPTIGHT is...

... climbing a mountain in Tibet to meditate, and then forgetting what you went up there for.

UPTIGHT is...

...discovering the flowers
in your hair attract wasps.

UPTIGHT is...

...looking around and seeing
Bert Parks at your "pot" party.

UPTIGHT is...

...contemplating your navel while on LSD, and
watching as your appendix starts coming out of it.

THE PUSHER'S SERENADE

*(Sung to the tune of
"I'll Be Seeing You")*

I'll be bleeding you
  With every fix that you are needing!
  At my feet you'll kneel there pleading
    All day through!
In the candy store
Behind the back-room door
  You'll spend your daddy's cash
  For acid trips,
  For pot and hash!

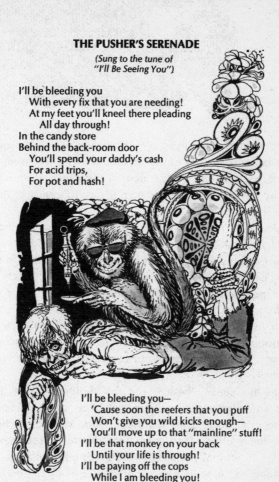

I'll be bleeding you—
  'Cause soon the reefers that you puff
  Won't give you wild kicks enough—
  You'll move up to that "mainline" stuff!
I'll be that monkey on your back
  Until your life is through!
I'll be paying off the cops
  While I am bleeding you!

"For every man whose career begins to flower,
there's another with poison envy!"
—Alfred E. Neuman

to enriching their lives. What you do with your own life is *not* a private matter that concerns only yourself. Because your life is intended to contribute to the life of humanity, to take your own life is, in effect, to take life from others.

And yet most of us undoubtedly are a lot more guilty of taking our own lives than of killing others. However, suicide is not the particular problem; most suicides probably are to be understood as the acts of sick people rather than as transgressions of the sixth commandment. The much more critical problem consists in the stupid things we do to ourselves, things we suppose will enhance life and add to its enjoyment when actually they hurt our capability to live as truly human.

In this sense, there is not the slightest doubt that the so-called mainline drugs kill their users. In some cases, of course, they kill them dead. More often they kill them alive—turn them into mental cases, make them emotionally incompetent, or simply get them so entangled in their habit that they are of no earthly good to themselves or to society. "The Pusher's Serenade" paints the picture with complete accuracy.

Regarding these mainline drugs, the evidence is obvious, conclusive, and widespread. Anybody who messes himself up with these, and then claims that

he didn't know they were dangerous, is probably guilty of violating the ninth commandment ("You shall not bear false witness") as well as the sixth. But what about pot—marijuana? Is the case the same here? Many young people insist that it is not.

Granted, there is a great deal we do not yet know about the bodily effects of pot smoking, so it may be that marijuana does not seriously damage one's physical or mental capabilities. But by the same token, we do not *know* for a fact that it is harmless.

"Pot is no worse than alcohol." Even if this were true—although we do not know that it is—it would not be much of a recommendation for pot. (Keep reading until we get to alcohol.) Physical deterioration is not the only way of losing life, and there are other considerations that qualify both pot and alcohol as killers.

"Smoking pot leads to the use of mainline drugs." It may be the case that there is no causative biochemical factor in pot that sucks one on into the hard drugs, but the statement has a great deal of truth in it anyhow. Once one is used to the idea of becoming high, it is just that much easier to accept other means of getting that way. The testimony of a great many addicts establishes the fact.

But the greatest killer threat involved in pot does

not lie in these areas where our knowledge is far from complete. The greater threat to true life and freedom lies in a realm beyond dispute. It is described in the words of a doctor who has worked with a number of young pot users:

"I'm troubled by the fact that so many bright and talented youngsters turn to marijuana as an escape from problem solving at a time when they should be learning to deal with life's stresses. Adolescence is a difficult period in which a young person must develop goals, stop depending on his parents, and learn to live with others. When a young person blunts this growing-up process with drugs, he is crippling his own personality development." *

Of course it is a bad scene for parents to go through the roof at the very mention of the word "pot"; but it is just as bad a scene for young people to pretend that the stuff presents no danger at all. That the parents may have chosen to kill themselves in their own way does not make it smart for the children to repeat the mistake. Perhaps **MAD,** with its serious yet not uptightly self-righteous satire, marks the best approach yet.

Although there still may be some open questions as to just how it does what it does, there is no longer any question at all but that tobacco is a killer—and that in a kill-'em-dead sense. There is no loophole left by which cigarette smoking can be excused or justified.

Before an assassin broke the sixth commandment to take his life, Senator Robert F. Kennedy spoke of the

* Quoted by Judith Ramsey, "Marijuana: Is it Worth the Risk?" *Family Health,* October 1969, p. 38.

Misery is...a cigarette...

TO A SHERIFF...

...It's a Top Gun's shot!

TO A RUSTLER...

...It's a Hangman's knot!

TO A COWBOY...

...It's a mad stampede!

TO A SMOKER...

...It's his weed!

145

TO A DIVER...

...it's a hungry shark!

TO A STROLLER...

...it's a Central Park!

TO A HUNTER...

...it's a charging stag!

TO A SMOKER...

...it's a drag!

TO A BIGOT...

...it's a Jew next door!

TO A KLANSMAN...

WE SHALL OVERCOME!

...it's a guy from CORE!

TO A BIRCHER...

...it's a Commie nut!

TO A SMOKER...

...it's a butt!

Art by Bob Clarke

TO A SMOKER...

... nicotine!

TO A DEEP CUT...

... it could be gangrene!

TO A WEAK HEART...

... it's some shocking news!

TO AN ULCER...

... it's a shot of booze!

♪ ♫ The taste ♪ That's what misery is!
The taste of death... ♪ ♫
The taste of death...

Presented as a Public Service by THE **K.E.N.T.*** SOCIETY

*"Knowledge Ends Needless Tumors"

147

If ever you're on the outskirts of Laredo,
Or any such town like that here in the West,
You'll see all the places we've planted young cowboys
Who died from those cigarette slugs in the chest!

Famous Marble-Row
Funereal Black

149

150

HECTOR J. QUINLEY

A CHAIN SMOKER FROM Shamokin, Pennsylvania

READ SO MUCH ABOUT

THE BAD EFFECTS OF SMOKING

... *THAT HE GAVE UP READING!*

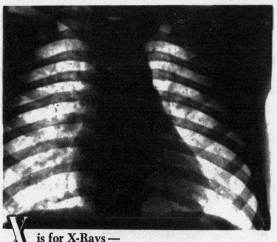

X is for X-Rays —
Our doctors are for them;
The cigarette firms would prefer
We ignore them!

"When it comes to hindsight, everybody's got 20-20 vision!"
—Alfred E. Neuman

151

assassin that breaks the commandment many times over: "At the present rate, one seventh of all Americans now alive—about 28 million people—will die prematurely of diseases associated with cigarette smoking. Every year cigarettes kill more Americans than were killed in World War I, the Korean War, and Vietnam combined. Each year cigarettes kill five times more Americans than traffic deaths do. The cigarette industry is peddling a deadly weapon. It is dealing in people's lives for financial gain."

Cigarettes are a bigger killer than either war or automobiles—and yet there is a difference in each case. Cigarettes are like automobiles in the sense that they cause death accidentally rather than deliberately. However, they are different from automobiles in the sense that they are in no way necessary to the life of society. It is one of the great stupidities of mankind that we allow cigarettes to be sold and used. And it is because **MAD** is so good at smelling out stupidities that it has done such a good job on tobacco. **MAD's** anti-cigarette ads (such as those on pages 145-49) are perhaps what they do best.

Goodness knows there are many smokers, such as the mother on page 150, who know what the score is and would like to stop but can't. I suppose they deserve some sort of sympathy. But a young person who knows what he is getting into and yet goes ahead and *starts* the habit—what's there to say about him?

Dr. A. Boone Doggle, professor of comparative anthropology at Lukadusgo University, Winston-Salem, North Carolina, had just returned from a research expedition to Nigeria and was regaling a class with his adventures. There was one incident he thought particularly revealing of the sublime gnorance and disinterestedness with which primitive people greet scientific knowledge.

One of the serious health threats in parts of rural Nigeria is the guinea worm, an intestinal parasite that gains entrance to the body through polluted drinking water. The larvae of the worm are too small to be readily visible, but they are large enough that they can be eliminated simply by straining the water through a cloth. Nigerian families and indeed entire communities could rid themselves of the infestation if the women would follow the simple expedient of straining the drinking water.

Educators, missionaries, public health officials, and all such authorities of course have tried hard to teach the villagers this simple measure for preserving health —but without notable success. The people just can't comprehend how they can be hurt by something they cannot see.

Dr. Doggle laughed at such primitive stupidity.

The class laughed, too—at Dr. Doggle. For they could *see* the cigarette he smoked as he told his story.

Research Question: Which is the greater health menace in the world today—guinea worms or tobacco? Who is justified at laughing at whose stupidity?

MAD's
GREAT MOMENTS IN ADVERTISING

the day no one was left up
to get him a Grant's

154

ONE
DAY
LAST
SUMMER

FWISK
GLURK

May You Be Filled With Christmas Spirit

SCHENLEY DISTILLERS Co.

THE SONG OF WINE-LOVERS

(Sung to the tune of "Hello, Young Lovers")

Hello, wine-lovers, whoever you are!
I hope your cellars are stocked!
Suavely you sip in your elegant style—
While you get suavely crocked!

Be sure, wine-lovers, whatever you do!
Be sure your wine is well-racked!
Smoothly inspect both the label and year—
While you get smoothly swacked!

You always show class
When you're sipping a glass
Of imported sauternes that you've poured!
You look so genteel
While you neatly conceal
That you're smashed—and drunk as a lord!

Beware, wine-lovers, whatever you do!
Beware your vice isn't known!
Let all the clods drink the booze and the beer!
You'll have a buzz of your own!
You'll have a buzz of your own on wine!
You'll have a buzz of your own!

If **ROBERT W. SERVICE** had written
LITTLE BOY BLUE

A bunch of the cows were mooing it up
    in the cornfield, so they tell;
And down in the meadow a big flock of sheep
    were raising a bit of hell;
There wasn't a way on that God-awful day
    of stopping that crop-wrecking crew—
'Cause under a haystack, flopped out on his back,
    lay that gold-bricking Little Boy Blue!

The folks from the farm, they all cried with alarm
    on that sad but sunny morn;
Each one of them knew he could save all their crops
    if he'd only blow his horn;
But none of them dared or especially cared
    to waken him from his snooze;
'Cause Little Boy Blue was as drunk as a skunk
    from a bottle of two-dollar booze!

The Barflies' Hymn

(to the tune of "*Over Hill, Over Dale*")

Over booze, over beer,
We will argue through the year
As the barflies go yapping along;
Football facts, baseball lore,
We remember every score,
As the barflies go yapping along;
   For it's Hi, Hi, Hee!
When some rummy don't agree—
Shout out your answer loud and strong:
    Sez You!
We will prove our point
While we're busting up the joint
As the barflies go yapping along!

What would be a lot smarter than kids all the time telling their parents, "Pot isn't any worse than alcohol" (meaning that therefore pot is OK), would be for them to tell the folks, "Pot is no better than alcohol" (meaning that we would all be better off by leaving both alone).

Actually, it is easier to document the case that alcohol is a killer than that marijuana is; alcohol has been around long enough and used widely enough to make statistical evidence abundant and available.

Look, then, at these figures. In this nation we spend $13 billion a year on booze. The expense of controlling the aftereffects (i.e., law enforcement, mental care, etc.) costs more than the liquor itself. The absenteeism and impaired work capability that result cost American industry another $4-7 billion annually. It is impossible, of course, to put a price on the lives that are taken or damaged, but even in sheer monetary outlay alcohol costs us a staggering sum—more than it takes to fight the Vietnam war, more than we ever would think of investing in something worthwhile, say, like education.

And it is not as though we were getting a return for this money. At most it buys a little short-term pleasure; in fact it buys a lot of long-term misery. When one considers what this kind of money could do in feeding hungry people, wiping out ghettos, or fighting air pollution, it must be obvious that to pour these funds down the drain of liquid enjoyment is, in all seriousness, to deprive many people of the life that could be theirs.

But this is only the beginning of the life that gets taken. Some 6.5 million American citizens suffer from alcoholism, a disease that drops one's potential for true humanity to almost zero. Through drinking, millions more, occasionally and to a lesser degree, drop their humanity in ways that affect their personality, health, good sense, and ability to operate. Some people, of course, actually kill themselves dead with the stuff.

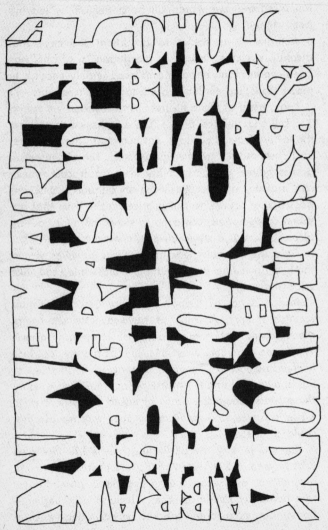

You Shall Not Kill

But the end is not yet. Liquor takes another big toll by causing some people to take life from others. As we observed earlier, at least 50 percent of all fatal highway accidents involve drinking drivers—and that's a lot of murder. Liquor contributes more than its share to the crime rate of the nation. Forty percent of all arrests are for drunkenness and drunk driving. One estimate suggests that considerably more than two thirds of the people arrested for felonies are under the influence of alcohol.

A Chicago judge is of the opinion that at least 33 percent of all child delinquency comes about because of drinking parents. And there is no knowing how much family tension and how many actual divorces are attributable to drink! How many friendships have been wrecked—or dehumanizing friendships made—through liquor? How many opportunities have been blown, how many vital decisions muffed, because, thanks to alcohol, a thinker didn't have his brain working as well as it should have been?

The picture would seem to be rather clear, wouldn't it? This stuff is nothing to play around with. Yet play around with it we do—gallon after gallon after gallon. We do it because we feel free; we do it in order to feel freer. But the sixth commandment says that free men shall not kill; anyone who uses his freedom to restrict the life either of himself or of others is not *using* his freedom—he is squandering it and dropping himself into slavery.

And that's why it is called firewater (see page 155). But why not? *Molotov* cocktails have not killed nearly as many people as other cocktails have; the Molotovs are safer by far.

The Fat Men's Chorus

(to the tune of "Stouthearted Men")

Give me some men
Who are fat-bellied men
Who will fight for their right to be slim!
Large, hulking slobs
Who will work off their blobs
In a pool, on a track, in a gym—*ugh!*
Grunting and huffing
And wheezing and puffing
They run and they jump and they swim!
When—
They've taken off two pounds
And shout how good they feel,
Then—
Fat-bellied men
Go home and eat a six-course meal!

"When it comes to absorbing information, some people are like blotters: they soak it all in, but they get it all backwards!"—Alfred E. Neuman

"The longer you nurse a grudge, the longer it takes to get better!"—Alfred E. Neuman

166

THE ICE CREAM PARLOR POLKA

(Sung to the tune of "Surrey With The Fringe On Top")

Every day is really a fun day
When I eat a big gooey sundae—
When I eat a big gooey sundae
With the nuts on top!

Cara-mel sauce all gluey and gummy!
Blobs of cream all tasty and yummy!
Gobs of fudge that drop in my tummy
With a slow plip-plop!

A cherry's a-sittin' on a pineapple slice!
The marshmallow syrup's all sticky!
The strawberry mixin' with the fudge real nice—
Which may be why I'm feelin' icky!

Though my figure's taking a beating
From this glob of goo that I'm eating—
When I'm through, you'll find me repeating
'Cause I just can't stop
Eating all those gooey sundaes
With the nuts on the top!

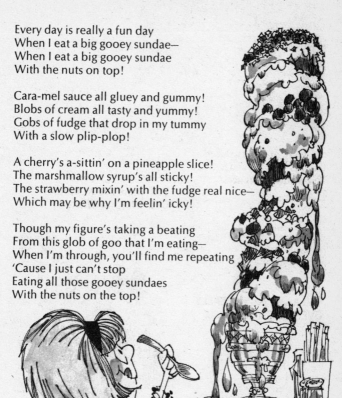

You Know You're REALLY OVERWEIGHT When...

... you can make a sloppy knot in your tie, and nobody knows the difference!

You Know You're REALLY OVERWEIGHT When...

... kids try to make you laugh so they can watch your tummy jiggle!

You Know You're REALLY OVERWEIGHT When...

... you feel that anything under a quarter isn't worth stooping to pick up.

Dope, tobacco, liquor—these all are things we would be better off without. They do more damage than any good that can be hoped from them; the misery they cause far outweighs any enjoyment they give. As far as concerns them, total abstinence, avoiding them completely, is the only way to fly—for birdmen who truly are free, who truly do not want to kill.

There are some other things in life, however, which are good and even necessary in themselves when used in moderation, but which become killers when used unwisely and not well.

MAD pictures just one of these on the preceding pages; the name of this poison is *food*. Mankind has used it to break the sixth commandment two ways at once. It took some doing, but modern man has managed. Many people have been killed by our not getting enough food to them to sustain life. That is tragic. But at the same time, many people also have killed themselves by eating too much food. Crazy, man, crazy! But also tragic, man, tragic! How unfree man is to take one of God's good gifts, bread, the very staff **of** *life*, and use it so stupidly that it kills.

And we do this with more than just food. Too little work kills—or at least "takes life" in the sense of wasting it in idleness and unproductiveness. Too much work kills. In our society we take life in both of these ways and double the sin-value of breaking one commandment.

Too little exercise can kill; and so can too much exertion. Too much sleep takes life by wasting it; too little takes life by starving it. Too little or no medicine at the time it is needed kills by failing to preserve life; drugs and medicines used wrongly or for the wrong purposes kill by destroying life.

The upshot of the matter is that health **is** life—which immediately puts health under the jurisdiction of the sixth commandment. "You shall not kill" now must mean—in addition to all the other meanings we have piled on it—"You shall so protect your health that you will not be guilty of taking your own life, but will preserve it as a contribution and service to the life of mankind."

The sixth commandment is the briefest of the commandments and it prohibits killing, but we have used it to kill 64 pages, one fourth of this book. **MAD**, man, **MAD!**

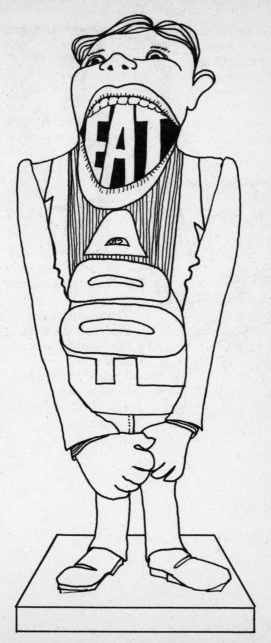

In Winter, Summer,
Fall and Spring,
some funny things
are happening.

IRVING'S
Furs

There is this thing:
She's called a Wife.
She loves a Husband
all her life.
There is this Husband
loved by her,
who's bringing her
a fancy fur.

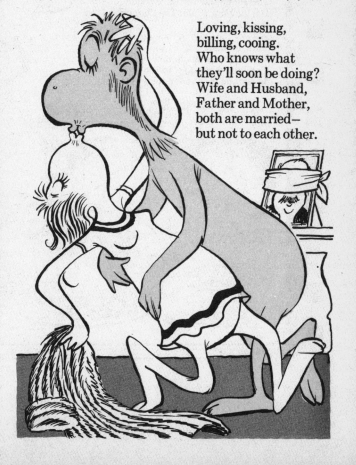

Loving, kissing,
billing, cooing.
Who knows what
they'll soon be doing?
Wife and Husband,
Father and Mother,
both are married—
but not to each other.

Lesson 4.

FUN AND GAMES

In each suburban community,
There is one indispensible man.
Is it the Mayor? No! The Clergyman? No!
It is the Caterer.
Without the Caterer, there would be no parties.
Then husbands and wives
Would have to talk to each other.
They would really get to know each other.
So you see, the Caterer holds the family together!

174

There are always parties in the suburbs.
There are teenage parties,
And there are grownup parties.
There is wild dancing and wild kissing
And plenty of liquor and plenty of drunks.
And the grownup parties are even more fun!
The grownups play games.
These games cause lots of laughs.
These games also cause lots of divorces!

VII
YOU SHALL NOT COMMIT ADULTERY

Question: How much does this commandment include under the word "adultery"?

Inevitably this is the first, last, and usually the only question in which people are interested. Does it include premarital sex relations? Does it include homosexuality and other abnormal sex behavior? Or does it refer only to adultery in the strict sense, to violations of the marriage contract—the kind noted here by **MAD**.

An honest examination of the evidence indicates that the original commandment did not cover even as much as is included in our word "adultery." Remember that, in the time of Moses, polygamy still was an accepted practice. A man could have as many wives as he could manage. Also it was acceptable for him to have relations with his concubines and/or slave girls, as it was with a girl to whom he was betrothed. None of these situations would have been termed adulterous. But more, the commandment probably was not intended to outlaw sexual relations between either single men and women or a married man and an unmarried girl (except, catch this, as it represented the making free with the property of the girl's father, the property being, of course, the girl herself). In short, unmarried women were fair game.

Hallelujah! This is the word we've been waiting to hear. The Ten Commandments envisioned a rather permissive society—and this means that there is nothing wrong with our having a permissive society now.

Wait a minute! Before you get so eager to jump to conclusions, it might be well to examine just where this Hebrew permissiveness came from and what it represented. All of the permissive practice described above was based upon the premise that women don't count. The assumption goes so far as to maintain that in sexual infidelity only men *can be* wronged; it is impossible even to talk about wronging a woman, because women have no rights to begin with. Thus, let a man collect as many wives, concubines, and slaves as he wants and use them as he will, none of these girls has any complaint coming; they are only women. Does a woman have the privilege of getting a little sexual variety in her turn? Not on your life; that would be an affront against the man to whom she belongs.

Likewise, for a wife to cheat on her husband is to do him a gross wrong. But when a man cheats on his wife, the only person wronged is the other woman's husband (or, if she is a young unmarried girl, her father). So if anyone desires to make something out of the permissiveness of the seventh commandment, he also is going to have to buy the women-are-dirt idea on which it is based—and that, obviously, won't go in this day and age.

Actually, the idea didn't last very long in Israel either. Although the likelihood is that he wrote some two or three centuries after the time of the commandments, the author of the Adam and Eve story is intent to make it absolutely clear that in the very creation of the world God designed things so that the only satisfactory human arrangement is that one man and one woman come together in a relationship that excludes all others:

"Then the man said,

'This at last is bone of my bones
and flesh of my flesh;
she shall be called Woman,
because she was taken out of Man.'

Therefore a man leaves his father and his mother and cleaves to his wife, and they become one flesh." (Genesis 2:23-24.)

Fortunately, the wording of the seventh commandment was flexible enough to include this more mature understanding of the nature and role of women. There is sufficient biblical evidence to indicate that Israel soon expanded her reading of the seventh commandment's word "adultery" to make it include any and all sexual activity outside the bounds of the marriage relationship.

Sorry, but there is nothing here that can be used to promote the idea of a permissive society. If that is what you have in mind, you would do well to go to *Playboy* rather than the Bible.

What Is A Make-Out Man?

WRITER: ARNIE KOGEN

ARTIST: SERGIO ARAGONES

BETWEEN the time of his first "Spin-The-Bottle" kissing game, and the time when, at the age of 81, he is hauled into court on "Bigamy" charges, you are guaranteed to come across a creature known as a "Make-Out Man". Make-Out Men come in four basic styles: "Hand-Holder", "Ear-Nibbler", "Hip-Hugger" and "Argentine Back-Breaker".

A MAKE-OUT Man can be seen anywhere: Crammed into a phone booth with 33 co-eds, making love at a drive-in movie (without even being in the car), dimming the lights at a fraternity party, giving mouth-to-mouth resuscitation on the beach (to a girl who hasn't been near the water), organizing a campus "Love-In", and playing "Simon Sez" at a Nudist Colony.

179

A MAKE-OUT Man is never a lighthouse keeper, an interior decorator, a librarian, an aluminum storm-door salesman, a ballet dancer, or a Boy Scout troop leader. He is always a bronzed Malibu surfer, a winner of a Marcello Mastroianni Look-Alike Contest, an Ohio State middle linebacker, a judge at the "Miss Bayonne, New Jersey, Beauty Pageant", a dance instructor at a Summer Resort, or a sitar player with a Raga Rock group.

A MAKE-OUT Man is Aggressiveness in a string of borrowed Love Beads, Vanity in a Dippity-do pompadour, Boldness cowering in a Vassar Dorm, Gentleness wrestling in a parked car, and Sincerity whispering, "This isn't just a Summer thing, baby! I promise I'll call you in the city!"

IT'S easy to spot a Make-Out Man. He has that one, unique identifying trademark that separates him from the rest of us clods . . . the "Make-Out Line." From coast to coast, you'll hear him uttering such classic phrases as: "Hi! You live around here?", "Don't I know you from someplace?", "Gosh, I never felt this way about any girl before!", "This time, it's the real thing!", "My place or yours?" and the ever-popular "Believe me, baby, I'll still respect you!"

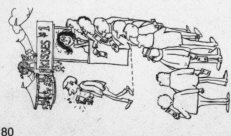

IF you date a Make-Out Man, you can't win. Nobody else is so slow to pick up a check or so quick to go "Dutch". Nobody else gets thrown out of movie balconies for "heavy breathing". Nobody else can ruin your reputation by merely being seen with you. And nobody else can kiss you so passionately that you have to be cooled off afterwards in a bath of cracked ice.

THE Make-Out Man is not a modern phenomenon. He has been with us throughout history. He was the guy who sweet-talked Betsy Ross into delaying the American Flag while she knitted him a pair of argyle socks. He was the guy who told Florence Nightingale, "Aw, don't give me that! I know all about you nurses!" He was the guy who, in 1513, whispered, "Look, let him go to Florida! We'll swing while he's gone!", to Mrs. Ponce De Leon.

MAKE-OUT Men are never named Sidney or Sol or Arnold or Jerome or Egbert. They are always named Porfirio or Lance or Marcello or Helmut or Tyrone. But strangely enough, they all seem to end up marrying girls named Zelda.

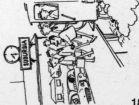

THERE are two types of Make-Out Man. The sophisticated Make-Out Man comes on strong with: Dinners by candlelight, soft music, moonlight walks, quoting from the philosophy of Kahlil Gibran, putting two cigarettes in his mouth and lighting them and then handing one to the girl, sending a bottle of wine to her table at a French restaurant, drinking champagne from her slipper, and taking her to the Senior Prom in a Cadillac convertible. The UNsophisticated Make-Out Man tries to score with: Lunches at McDonalds, country & western music, 12-mile hikes, quoting from the philosophy of Tony Curtis, putting two cigarettes in his mouth and then lighting his nose, sending a bowl of barley soup to her table at a Dairy restaurant, drinking Fresca from her golashe, and taking her to the Senior Prom in a rented Chicken Delight truck.

A MAKE-OUT Man is invariably a brazen "con artist". Who else would tell every date that his appendicitis scar is actually a Heidelberg dueling scar? Who else would take a girl into a neighborhood malt shop and order "One aphrodisiac with two straws!"? Who else would get thrown out of school for cheating . . . with the Dean's wife? Who else would say, "Oops, we're out of gas!" and then start necking . . . in the Lincoln Tunnel?

A MAKE-OUT Man is always in demand, and by everyone. Teeny-Boppers long to hold his warm hands, Career Girls desire to kiss his cool lips, Co-Eds yearn to nuzzle his soft neck, Older Women ache to fondle his strong chin, and Other Guys want to punch his silly face.

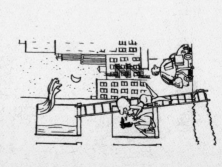

BUT above all, the Make-Out Man possesses the one trait that keeps him a cut above the regular clods at school, office or cocktail party . . . the one item that is more important than his charm or his looks or his fat address book or his ability to "dip" at a dance . . . that thing called "Confidence"! It is this invaluable confidence that once enabled a famous Make-Out Man who had reached the age of 101 to marry a girl of 19, and who, when his doctor advised him against it, saying, "There is such a vast age difference, it could mean . . . death!", replied with the words that have become "Classic" in the annals of Make-Outdom:

"WELL, IF IT DOES, I'LL JUST HAVE TO LOOK FOR ANOTHER WIFE!"

"Familiarity breeds attempt!"—Alfred E. Neuman

Boy! Invite a bunch of teenage boys to a backyard barbecue and under cover of darkness, they turn out to be nothing but **animals!**

Men are **all alike!** All they want to do is satisfy their **primitive urge!**

You'd think girls were made for nothing else but **that!**

They're **all hands** and **mouth!**

It's **disgusting!** They're interested in **one** thing, and one thing **only!**

FOOD!

"Bachelors, like detergents, work fast and leave no rings!"
—Alfred E. Neuman

AT HOME WITH THE "STARS"

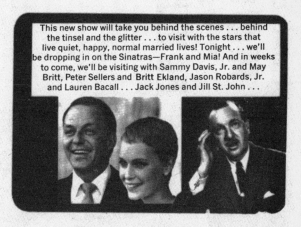

This new show will take you behind the scenes . . . behind
the tinsel and the glitter . . . to visit with the stars that
live quiet, happy, normal married lives! Tonight . . . we'll
be dropping in on the Sinatras—Frank and Mia! And in weeks
to come, we'll be visiting with Sammy Davis, Jr. and May
Britt, Peter Sellers and Britt Ekland, Jason Robards, Jr.
and Lauren Bacall . . . Jack Jones and Jill St. John . . .

A MAD Look At
HUGH
vs.
HELEN

Hugh Hefner tells his Playboy pals
How red to paint the town,
But Helen sells the Gurley gals
On doing it up Brown!

Hugh has his Bunnies gather for
The Key white-collar men,
But Helen's ploys are rather more,
Well, Cosmopolitan.

He bares The Naked and The Bed,
A Hymn to pretty Her;
But She proves with a two-page spread
The Nitty-Grittier.

He leads his flock, the Churchmen chide,
    Along the Devil's way,
But She is on the Angel's side,
    Exhorting, "Let Us PREY!"

Hugh's views on double pleasure shared
    By giving sex a whirl,
Are only child's Play, Boy, compared
    To Helen's "Single Girl."

WRITER: RONNIE NATHAN
ARTIST: JACK RICKARD

191

Sex is fun; the activity is enjoyable. The Bible doesn't deny it; and it didn't take Hugh Hefner or Helen Gurley Brown to discover it. Lots and lots of people knew it already.

But lots and lots of people also knew of something that is lots more fun, longer lasting fun, and more dependable fun: this is not simply sex, but sex in marriage. By marriage, it must be said, we do not have in mind just each and every arrangement that has been legalized by a wedding license, but only those that the Genesis author could describe as a becoming of "one flesh," a merging of total interests, welfare, and concerns.

Sex is frosting; marriage (true marriage) is cake. Frosting is good; cake is good; but frosted cake is much better than either alone; they are made for each other.

The trouble with frosting eaters and those who can't wait until they have a cake before they start tasting frosting is that they cannot properly learn to digest cake and so appreciate the superior pleasure of frosted cake. Even when they have a cake (or the makings of a cake) many of them have such a craving to do frosting-tasting that their cake never gets made, and the rib-tickling goodness of frosted cake never gets experienced.

When a young person is just dying to taste frosting, but has very little concept of what cake can be, it is very difficult to convince him that the matter is as we have described it. Why can't he eat frosting now and frosted cake if and when it comes along? After all, the product that is being huckstered so effectively by the likes of Hugh and Helen, by movies like *The Sandpiper* (page 187), by TV shows like *Peyton Place* (page 188), and by all the other mass media, is frosting, not frosted cake.

Yet there is plenty of experience to indicate that the eating of frosting by itself causes bellyaches. Unwanted pregnancies and venereal disease make up only a small part of the pain. The fact that most people have been taught and instinctively know the truth of what we have been saying about frosted cake gives them pangs of guilt and remorse when they deliberately ignore their consciences. But by far the greater hurt comes in impairing one's capability for the most satisfying sort of marriage. Any number of studies have shown that those who wait for frosted cake make better marriage partners than those who do not.

The make-out man (pages 179-83) and the gal who advertises like "that kind of a girl" (page 185) may get their kicks for the moment, but they are a poor bet for the race (the human race) that is in it for the long haul and for some accomplishments more important than mere explosions of ecstasy.

194

In our day and age, it is difficult enough to create strong, stable families that provide happiness and worthwhileness for both parents and children—let alone saddling society with the extra handicap of trying to build those families out of frosting tasters. Even in the semi-permissive society that we have had up to the present, we have been beset with the sort of marital conflict that produces the agonies of lovelessness, divorce, neglected and twisted children, violence, alcoholism, and who knows what all. What, really, do Hugh Hefner and Helen Gurley Brown think we would be in for if society went as permissive as they advocate?

With the seventh commandment as clearly as with any of them, the issue is freedom. Use your freedom for all-out sex, the commandment says, and you blow your long-term freedom to create and enjoy one of life's greatest experiences, the becoming of one flesh for which man was created. Just as Israel discovered that sexual permissiveness needed to be severely checked if women were to find their place as true human beings, it may be that modern man will need to learn the same lesson if any of us are to have the chance of becoming truly human.

VIII

YOU SHALL NOT STEAL

This undoubtedly is the one commandment of the ten that is least relevant to life today.

"You mean that stealing isn't a problem? You must be **MAD**!"

No, that is not what I mean. I mean that the commandment originally may have said something quite different than it does today. The problem is that the Hebrew word for "covet" (in the tenth commandment) seems, in Moses' day, to have been almost synonymous with the word for "steal" used here. In this case, the eighth and the tenth commandments are for all practical purposes identical. The eighth says, "You shall not steal (period)"; the tenth says, "You shall not steal this and this and this and this." And obviously, either God or Moses could have done a better job of composing commandments than that.

Consequently, some scholars think that the eighth commandment originally included an additional

THE INEXPENSIVE HANDYMAN
(Fixit Domesticus)

NATURAL HABITAT

The "Fix-Up-And-Make-Do" *Inexpensive Handyman* was usually spotted in a cluttered-up little shop, knee-deep in broken vacuum cleaners, pop-up toasters, electric fans and clocks.

RECOGNIZABLE FEATURES

He was easily identified by the pencil behind his ear, the screwdriver jutting out of his bulging pockets, and the old oil-stained overalls upon which he wiped his greasy hands.

CHARACTER TRAITS

He was known to take a modest pride in his ability to save a customer money by improvising a part to replace the one no longer made for an out-moded but well-built appliance.

USUALLY HEARD SAYING:

"Shucks, I should pay YOU for giving me a chance to work on this wonderful old thing. A buck-and-a-half is plenty!"

The **"INEXPENSIVE HANDYMAN"** is rapidly being replaced by:

198

THE SPECIALIZED SERVICE TECHNICIAN
(Con Jobus Maximus)

NATURAL HABITAT

The modern "Fast-Buck" *Service Technician* is usually found on a job with his head buried in a copy of "Playboy" while being paid by the hour—or, if he is self-employed, boxing several supposedly "defective" parts he's removed from one appliance—to be installed as "new" when servicing another.

RECOGNIZABLE FEATURES

He is easily identified by the bill he presents containing illegibly-scrawled double-talk and a huge "Service Charge".

CHARACTER TRAITS

He is known to talk like an expert on sports, politics and world affairs (—or anything but his own field!) to keep a customer from asking questions he really couldn't answer.

USUALLY HEARD SAYING:

"It's in pretty bad shape! It's gotta go back to the shop!"

phrase. If one runs through the inventory of items listed under the tenth commandment, it rather clearly is seen to include everything that possibly could be stolen from an Israelite householder—with one exception. The exception is the householder himself. There is a real possibility, then, that in its earliest form the eighth commandment read: "You shall not steal a man" (or "an Israelite man"; or "your neighbor"). The meaning, of course, would have been that you should not kidnap your neighbor to make him a slave or sell him into slavery.

Under such a reading the final five commandments would form a very logical and natural sequence: namely, regarding your neighboring householder, you shall not threaten his life (kill), his marriage (adultery), his freedom (steal him), his reputation (false witness), or his property (covet, i.e. steal, his belongings).

But the eighth commandment has lost its final phrase, and the explanation seems quite apparent. There is evidence within the Old Testament itself to indicate that the Hebrew word used in the tenth commandment gradually changed its meaning into what accurately is communicated by our word "covet." Now the eighth and tenth commandments were no longer repetitious (the eighth prohibited the outward act of robbery and the tenth prohibited the inward impulse of selfish desire), and, obviously, by dropping the final phrase, the eighth should be extended to cover all stealing rather than just kidnapping.

Because **MAD** has plain failed to comment on the problem of people making off with their neighbors and selling them in the slave auction, we have no alternative but to make the same change that the Bible itself made. Our topic will be "stealing," pure and simple (or in whatever other forms it appears).

The observation impressed upon us by our illustrations from **MAD** is that more stealing goes on through legal means than through the illegal means of undisguised theft and robbery. This, of course, is not to excuse the thievery of thieves, but to alert us to the subtler forms of stealing into which many of us "honest men" can slip without our even admitting that it is stealing. But **MAD** knows what it is and says so.

Much of this stealing, **MAD** suggests, goes on under the cover of "shrewd business practice." The point, of course, is not that all mechanics, toy manufacturers, or appliance repairmen are thieves, or even that more thievery goes on in these businesses than others. **MAD** is very generous as regards the variety of businesses it is willing to take on; we have selected only a few pages. But the point is that the stealing disease can and does infect all types of business. We need to watch out that we do not get took; but more, we need to watch ourselves that we do not become guilty of violating the eighth commandment.

The Cheater's Chant

(to the tune of "Bless 'em All")

Cheat 'em all!
Cheat 'em all!
In Springtime, in Winter and Fall!
Those Lincoln quotations we hide in our fist!
That Longfellow verse written on our left wrist!
If you find that your mind can't recall
The date when the Romans took Gaul—
A glance at your knee-cap
Will help you to recap!
So why take a chance?
Cheat 'em all!

O O O
LICENSE TO STEAL

Issued To

WILLIAM M. GAINES

Publisher Of MAD

This license permits the holder to ask the ridiculous sum of 30¢ for a collection of inane articles like this one, and also allows him to ask the even more ridiculous sum of 50¢ when such garbage is reprinted.

The topic still is stealing, but with this page it is brought closer home for most readers. **MAD** is not content to leave the matter by pointing out the stealing that the evil adults do. The kids know that all those people are no good to begin with—that's the name of the generation gap game today. But **MAD** has some things to say about stealing done even by the oh-so-moral youth generation.

The form that most of this stealing takes is "cheating." You know how much of that goes on better than I do.

But what is stolen and who is stolen from when cheating takes place in the schoolroom?

I am myself a teacher and, paraphrasing Shakespeare, can say without fear of contradiction, "Who steals my grades steals trash." The grades did not belong to me in the first place, and I am none the poorer for having them stolen. So who stole what from whom?

The cheater steals from his classmates and predominantly from himself. By taking a grade higher than what he deserved, he is devaluating the significance of all the grades in the class and thus stealing from those who earned their grades honestly. Perhaps the honest students who allow the cheaters to copy their work would not be so willing to have this happen if they realized that they were harming their own grades—and also encouraging the teacher to make the next exam harder in order to get the grade distribution more accurate.

Most of all, however, the cheater steals from himself. The taxpayers, his parents, and (in the case of many college students) the student himself lay out considerable sums of money for schooling. More to the point, the student invests a great deal of his own time and energy in the process. And what is the goal, the end product, of this expensive outlay and investment? An education, of course.

But the cheater has switched goals; he bypasses the education and goes for the grades and the diploma (which, in themselves, are the next thing to worthless). It is as if a food-packer filled a can wih garbage, labeled it as Grade A fruit cocktail—and then took it home and ate it himself. When one is working for oneself (which is what the educational process represents), it is just a little stupid to cheat your employer. The commandment shouldn't have to say it, but some people would do well to read it to mean, "You shall not steal from yourself."

Another theft is involved, too. As with the rest of the commandments, to break this one is to rob oneself of freedom. It is unrealistic to expect that a student can cheat with impunity in school and then suddenly upon graduation become an honest man in his business and other dealings. The school kids pictured on pages 202-04 of **MAD** grow up to be the ones pictured on the pages before and after; they steal from themselves the freedom of living as honest and upright men.

Confession is good for the soul. All this sermonizing about stealing leads (see License on page 205) to **MAD's** admitting the truth about itself (in fun, of course). But maybe the example can encourage us to get with it.

We confess that most of this book is stolen from **MAD**—not only the pages made up of material lifted directly, but also the ideas and inspiration for much of the text as well. The plan also has been to steal a little of **MAD's** reputation and goodwill for the selling of the book. All this stealing is with **MAD's** permission, of course; and we can't think of anyone we would rather steal from.

Our observations about the history and development of the Ten Commandments, we must also confess, have been stolen largely from two books. One is *The Ten Commandments in Recent Research* by Johann Jakob Stamm and Maurice Edward Andrew. The second is *The Ten Commandments in New Perspective* by Eduard Nielsen. Both books are part of the series "Studies in Biblical Theology" from the SCM Press of London, England. And now that we have recognized these sources, our stealing ceases to be stealing, for this is the way that scholarship operates.

DEAR
HONEYMOONERS—

Your wedding trip is over now;
  Your honeymoon is ended;
We're sure you liked your stop-off here
  And found the weather splendid;
By now, you must be settled down;
  Your brand-new home is started
With all those blankets, chairs and lamps
  You stole when you departed!

M A G N O L I A   M O T E L

The Taxpayers' Rouser

(to the tune of "The Song of the Vagabonds")

On—you big employers,
Clerks, and cooks and lawyers—
Cheat, cheat, cheat
    Your Uncle Sam!
With expenses padding
And exemptions adding,
Cheat, cheat, cheat
    Your Uncle Sam!
Don't declare the money that you earn!
Better still—don't file a return!
You'll be saving plenty,
And draw ten to twenty
Years in jail for Uncle Sam!

Don't You Hate . . . a date who orders the most expensive items on the menu, and then hardly eats anything!

"Whether a man winds up with a nest egg or a goose egg often depends upon the chick he marries!"—Alfred E. Neuman

Unfortunately, stealing is not confined to the shady practices of some businessmen and the cheating of some students; any of us can fall into it in many different ways. The **MAD** selections seen here present just a few examples.

Honeymooners shouldn't have to take all the blame, but motels, hotels, restaurants, and other businesses do lose a tremendous quantity of goods to common filchers. Most of these people, I suppose, look upon themselves as honest citizens—although it is rather difficult to understand how they justify that claim. Shoplifters don't get pictured here, but they pose a major problem for many retail businesses; and their doings have the effect of raising prices for the rest of us.

"The Taxpayers' Rouser" exposes a real sore point on stealing. It is amazing how many people—from the big oilmen with their depletion allowances to the small man with his income taxes—are willing to steal from their own government, cheat Uncle Sam, as the song has it. And many of these, I would guess, think of themselves as great patriots, have a flag decal on the car window and a sticker "America: Love It or Leave It" on the bumper.

The tiring satire of the kid attiring his car calls for no comment; that is the most obvious sort of theft. But, alongside, the slum landlord must be recognized as just as much a thief. Overpricing, wherever it occurs, is a violation of the eighth commandment.

The "Don't You Hate . . ." item introduces a totally new method of stealing—and one to which we ought to give careful thought. Why does the fellow hate this kind of a date? Because, in reality, she has stolen from him. He would have been happy to put out the moolah for the meal if she would have taken commensurate value and enjoyment out of it; but she, in effect, took his money without giving anything (even appreciation) in return. In truth, then, waste is theft. When anyone entrusts something to you and you fail to use it for the purpose for which it was entrusted, you have stolen that which he gave. Verily, the eighth commandment catches us all!

The TV Victim's Lament

(Sung to the tune of *"Blowin' in the Wind"*)

How many times must a guy spray with Ban
    Before he doesn't offend?
And how many times must he gargle each day
    Before he can talk to a friend?
How many tubes of shampoo must he buy
    Before his dandruff will end?
The sponsors, my friend, will sell you all they can.
    The sponsors will sell you all they can.

How many times must a man use Gillette
    Before shaving won't make him bleed?
And how many cartons of Kents must he smoke
    Before the girls all pay him heed?
How many products must one person buy
    Before he has all that he'll need?
The sponsors, my friend, will sell you all they can.
    The sponsors will sell you all they can.

How many times must a gal clean her sink
    Before Ajax scours that stain,
And how many times must she rub in Ben-Gay
    Before she can rub out the pain?
How many ads on TV must we watch
    Before we are driven insane?
The sponsors, my friend, will broadcast all they can.
    The sponsors will broadcast all they can!

217

By variously attributing his 38-point-per-game average of the previous season to the use of the proper shave cream, mouth wash, deodorant, wart-remover, crankcase additive, and kosher salami, Blaring set a League Record by earning $724,575 in product endorsements this year. He also set a League Record for having his per-game scoring average drop from 38 to 4 when TV commercial filming commitments made it inconvenient for him to attend practice sessions.

"Making out your Income Tax form
is like making out a laundry list
—either way, you lose your shirt!"
—Alfred E. Neuman

IX

YOU SHALL NOT BEAR FALSE WITNESS AGAINST YOUR NEIGHBOR

This is a good commandment, but it is a little too limited for our purposes. For one thing, it treats only one sort of falsehood, namely, that which defames the neighbor, the Israelite householder whose *reputation* (in this case) is not to be violated. For another thing, it covers only legal testimony, the sort of witnessing that transpires in a court of law.

As it stands, the commandment does not forbid any and all sorts of lying and deceit. However, it is perfectly proper to start where the commandment does and generalize the principle to apply to other situations. It is evident that this process takes place within the Bible itself. The commandment points toward a particularly crucial place for truth-telling—the situation in which a man's good name, his future, and perhaps his very life may hang on it—and the implication follows naturally that the same quality of truth-telling should prevail throughout every sphere of life.

We shall make free, then, to extend the commandment by dropping the final phrase and ignoring the law court particularity, thus having it read: "You shall not lie or deceive."

Actually, there is some advantage in the commandment's reading "bear false witness" rather than simply "lie." To lie refers almost too narrowly to "deliberately *speaking* false *words*." However, if we go beyond the legal context, "to bear false witness" can cover anything a person might say, do, or suggest with the intent of leading another to a conclusion that is anything less than true; it is very possible to bear false witness without actually lying at any point. In fact, it is precisely this sort of false witness that **MAD** wants to talk about; out-and-out big fat lying is too obvious and gross to require the services of **MAD's** talent for nosing out subtleties.

The **MAD** stuff seen here bears in on one of its favorite targets: advertising. Advertising is one of the largest and most influential industries in America; yet how far could it get without the bearing of false witness? For the most part it is not deemed necessary to use the outright lie; but encouraging people to draw conclusions which are not quite true is the very name of the game.

From one standpoint it could be argued that this sort of petty deceit is harmless. Everyone knows that advertising isn't intended as being the truth, the whole truth, and nothing but the truth. Indeed, the advertisers themselves don't expect most people to buy their whole gambit hook, line, and sinker. In other words, advertising becomes a kind of game in which neither the advertiser nor the public takes the other with complete seriousness.

However, the question is whether truth is something that ought to be played with in this fashion. It is a very dangerous game at best. The trouble is that people get confused as to just when the game is being played and when it is not—and the success of advertising lies precisely in people becoming thus confused.

Once get this game going in society and soon it becomes impossible to know when the game is on and when it is off, who is playing and who is not, where lies "in bounds" and where lies "out of bounds." Soon we wind up where we are today, with people not being able simply to accept as the truth whatever is presented as being true. Our society no longer does or can operate on the basis of mutual trust and reliance on the word of others. To this extent (and because we thus have broken the ninth commandment) we are not free.

How much freer we could be in all our relationships with one another if it were not necessary always to guard against the possibility that the other man might be bearing false witness! And how tragic that loss of freedom becomes when, because we know that this is the way the world runs, we become willing to play a little of the game ourselves. The ninth commandment (as all the others) is of vital importance for our life together; once we break it and forfeit our freedom, slavery becomes a vicious circle.

222

THE OLD-FASHIONED GRANDMOTHER
(Nana Affectionatus)

NATURAL HABITAT

The gentle *Old-Fashioned Grandmother* was most often seen near a stove, producing a variety of now-extinct foods— like fluffy home-made bread, fried chicken and gooey apple pie—all of which she was fond of sharing with young folks.

RECOGNIZABLE FEATURES

The "Granny" was easily identified by her billowing figure, her neat hair pulled back in a bun, her wrinkled face— free of greasy make-up, and her huge clean flowered apron.

CHARACTER TRAITS

She was never known to panic in an emergency; she believed that a woman's place was in the home; and she devoted her life to caring for her one mate—"THE RESPECTED GRANDPA".

USUALLY HEARD SAYING:

"Come in! I'm happy to see you! Have some Chicken Soup!"

The **"OLD-FASHIONED GRANNY"** is rapidly being replaced by:

THE FACE-LIFTED DOWAGER

(Haggus Neuroticus)

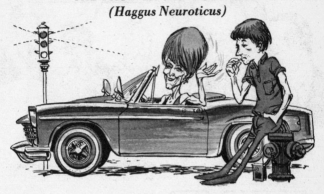

NATURAL HABITAT

The *Modern Grandmother* is usually found at resorts, bingo parlors or bars . . . any place but her home. Does not like to be seen with children who might call her "Grandma" or "Nana" or anything else that would disclose her real age.

RECOGNIZABLE FEATURES

She is easily identified by her scrawny, emaciated figure —the results of eating low-calorie, diet-fad foods—and her brilliantly colored and styled hair, which looks as if she's just left a Beauty Parlor—which, of course, she has.

CHARACTER TRAITS

She is known to panic and become unstrung whenever she is visited by grandchildren, resorting to tranquilizers until they leave. She often survives her mate, who is so bugged by her incessant nagging demands that he finally kicks off, leaving the huge insurance policy she now lives it up on.

USUALLY HEARD SAYING:

"Do you know, they think my daughter and I are Sisters?"

The Goof-Off's Anthem

(to the tune of **"Over Hill, Over Dale"**)

In a test
For a class
That we know that we can't pass—
See the goof-offs go faking along!

Start to heave;
Fake a chill;
Anything so you'll look ill;
As the goof-offs go faking along!

For it's hi-hi-hoo!
Let's all fake the Asian flu!
Call out your symptoms loud and strong—
"Blah! Ecch!"
We will feel enthused
When the teachers says "Excused!"
As the goof-offs go faking along!

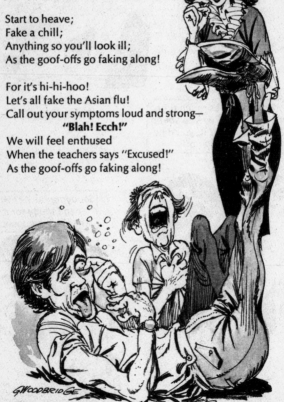

"People should stand on their own two feet!" said Hiram Judd, the President of the "Dirt Farmer's Anti-Welfare State Lobby," which marched on Washington to protest allocation of government funds for the underprivileged. Judd is also President of the "More Subsidies For Dirt Farmers Lobby."

Chapter Three

See the young man.
He is screaming.
Why is he screaming?
He feels he is being victimized by a Ruthless Power.
He feels he is being oppressed by a Military Aggressor.
He feels he is being enslaved by a Totalitarian Regime.
Is he a Czech Liberal?
Or a Hungarian Revolutionist?
No! The young man is an American Student.
He is a member of the "New Left".
But not for long.
Next year, he graduates.

Chapter 7.

See the Philanthropist.
He gives lots of money away.
Why does he give lots of money away?
Does his conscience tell him to do it?
No, his Accountant tells him to do it.
The money he gives away is "Tax-Deductible."
His tax-deductible contributions
Support Museums and Symphony Orchestras.
If he gave the same money in taxes,
It would support Schools and Hospitals.
When this Hypocrite gives away money,
He gets his name in the newspapers.
No one gets his name in the newspapers
For paying his taxes!

"The grass is always greener at the Golf Club that has a restricted membership!"—Alfred E. Neuman

233

YOU SHALL NOT BEAR FALSE WITNESS AGAINST YOUR NEIGHBOR

This business of bearing false witness can appear in almost any way, shape, or form—and **MAD** is good at spotting all of them. Indeed, the foregoing pages might indicate that the heart of the problem lies not so much in bearing false witness *against the neighbor* as in bearing false witness in *favor of oneself*. It may well be true that we work harder at trying to make ourselves look good than in trying to make the other fellow look bad; but it is false witness either way.

Page 222 opens where all good moral analysis should begin, namely with exposing the adults as the hypocrites that they are. (If you enjoyed that sentence you had better not look at pages 226-29: **MAD** is never content to stop without whacking at everybody in sight.)

One of the most popular false witnesses among adults these days, **MAD** knows, is to make as if one were younger, in better shape, and more "with it" than actually is the case. From the fellow on page 222 (Did Dave Berg mean for him to look that much like William Gaines, the **MAD** publisher? Just call him "Thin Ice Berg!") through the *Haggus Neuroticus (I* love that!) and Mrs. Size 12, the picture comes clear.

It is a picture that in many respects is humorous and sometimes pathetic, but it also is a picture that carries very serious implications. Many of the problems of interpersonal relations that plague our society can be traced to the older generation's refusal to face the fact that it is older. When parents (and grandparents) fight the truth of what they are and act as though they were less responsible teen-agers, it is no wonder that things get difficult. This is a type of false witness that our society can ill afford.

Don't go away; we need to look at pages 226-29. Perhaps there are some other people who are guilty of bearing false witness—like say, a fellow who would have his father believe that he had tried to get a job, one who would have his dad think that his deepest interest and concern was to do a good job on tomorrow's exam, the poor kids who have such an acute health problem, and the threesome who so want to do their bit in encouraging the beauty of humanity. No further comment is necessary.

Pages 230-233 home in on the thought of false witness that perhaps is not quite so innocent, and which with more justice can be branded as sheer hypocrisy. The intent now is not simply to look good but to reap a profit for oneself while looking good at the same time. A great deal of this sort of thing does go on; **MAD's** examples only scratch the surface. The ninth commandment may be the one that is least respected among us; we would do well to give it serious consideration.

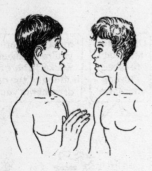

Mr. Kaputnik, would **you** drive me to the club? We're having a teenage dance...

So?! There's plenty of **public** transportation!

Yeah, but **you've** got an **eight thousand dollar sports car!** I wanna drive up in **style** so the other guys will be **impressed!**

Oh, so you're a **status-seeker!**

I'll tell you how to impress the other guys! Here's a **quarter!** Take the **"B" bus** to the club.

Then, you'll **really** drive up in style! The "B" bus costs **THIRTY THOUSAND DOLLARS!**

X
YOU SHALL NOT COVET

We have noted already (page 197) that the word here translated "covet" originally meant something closer to "steal," i.e., actually to take steps toward acquiring. However, even within biblical times the meaning of the term changed, and we choose to use it in the generally accepted second sense.

Now "to covet" refers to the inner desire that often leads to stealing—and to many other deplorable things. To covet is to want something you can't have (or shouldn't have) and want it so much that the very desire prevents your finding happiness with what you do have and in what you truly are.

This commandment is different than the other nine in focusing not upon outward, visible action and attitudes, but upon the inner motives that lie behind outward action. (It was precisely this uniqueness of the ninth commandment that led scholars into an examination of the word "covet.") However, as an inner motive, covetousness often moves one directly into transgression of other commandments—stealing, killing, adultery, the making of images, the worshiping of other gods, almost any of them.

And it is easy to see that freedom is *the* issue here. A person who wants something so bad he can taste it hardly is free to taste all the good and wonderful things that are already available to him. A covetous man is a man in jail; he can see freedom and there is nothing he wants more, but the bars prevent him from getting there. The difference is that the man in jail was thrown there by someone else, whereas the covetous man has built his own cage out of the bars of unrealistic and unhealthy desires. On the other hand, one of the freest men the world has ever seen was the apostle who, while sitting in a literal jail, nevertheless could write, "I have learned, in whatever state I am, to be content."

Anyone interested in being free and staying free, the commandment suggests, will do well not to covet.

Yet in our day and age, the problem of covetousness has been aggravated out of all proportion to what it must have been in Moses' day. With his people, one Hebrew hardly could possess much that any other Hebrew did not already have. Oh, one might have ten sheep while another had twenty—but make of them what you will, sheep are sheep and no great thing around which to build a case of covetousness. The entire community shared pretty much the same standard of living and enjoyed about equal opportunity.

But today . . . We have a technology that has created an infinity of things that people want. We have an advertising industry to make people want them ("them" including things like sex, glamor, status, and prestige as well as simply material possessions). We have an affluence that tempts people into thinking that all these things are within their reach. And above all, we have a mentality which assumes that a man has some sort of God-given right to do *whatever is necessary* to make himself happy, the right to become whatever and whoever he decides he wants to be. Put them all together, they spell *covetousness,* the hallmark of our society.

MAD knows what the situation is. **MAD** knows that, in this regard, the only difference between the youth and the adult generation is that they covet somewhat different things. And Dave Berg's is the pen that stabs this insight home with a thrust that may go deep enough to make a difference. Perhaps the commandment against covetousness should have been the first one rather than the last; if we were to obey the covetousness-curbing commandment, all the rest would go much easier.

BALLAD FOR A MINK COAT

(Sung to the tune of
"The Girl That I Marry")

The mink I'm possessing,
It's plain to see,
Has given me su-per-i-or-i-ty!
Those gorgeous, costly pelts
Convince me I'm better than anyone else!
My friends flock around me when I stroll by!
They look at my coat with a jealous eye!
I'm concealing—
Not revealing—
With a second-hand Thrift-Shop I'm dealing!
A coat for impressing
The mink I'm possessing
Will be!

ANTHEM FOR AN OVEN

(Sung to the tune of
"I'm Looking Over A Four-Leaf Clover")

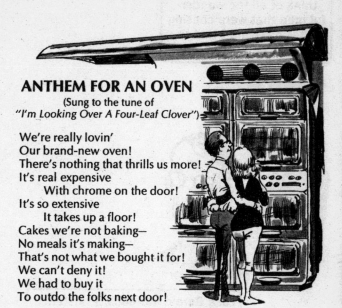

We're really lovin'
Our brand-new oven!
There's nothing that thrills us more!
It's real expensive
    With chrome on the door!
It's so extensive
    It takes up a floor!
Cakes we're not baking—
No meals it's making—
That's not what we bought it for!
We can't deny it!
We had to buy it
To outdo the folks next door!

HYMN TO A RICH AUNT

(Sung to the tune of
"You're A Grand Old Flag")

She's a mean old bag!
She's a nasty old bag!
And forever she's filled us with hate!
    But we treat her sweet
    And kiss her feet
And tell her we think that she's great!

Let her curse at us!
We will not raise a fuss
When she starts in to scream and nag!
For we all are counting what we'll get
From the will of that mean old bag!

245

246

FREEDOM NEEDS FENCES

The title above is not intended to say that freedom must be restricted; it is intended to say that freedom cannot maintain itself *as freedom* without the help of boundaries.

Child psychologists have discovered that small children feel more secure (and thus more free) when playing in a fenced yard than in one that has no limits. The fences help the child know *where* his freedom lies; he knows how far he can exercise freedom without it threatening to change into lostness. Assuredly, a lost person is not a free person; and even the fear of becoming lost can severely restrict one's capacity for free action. The child understands the fence more as a guarantee of freedom than as a threat to it.

If adults were willing to confess their own childlikeness, they would see that the principle also applies to them. Fences (the right kind of fences in the right kind of places) make for freedom.

The idea can be demonstrated from many realms.

Automobile traffic can move freely only with the aid of boundaries, namely, the lines between lanes (particularly the two lanes that run in opposite directions) and also the edges (the very lineality of the highway itself, which rather than spreading out every which way, is bounded so as to run in a given direction). Imagine a city in which the buildings were placed at random, all the intervening space asphalted, and the cars turned loose to go where they would. Theoretically this would be freedom—freedom both for the builders who could build wherever they choose and for the drivers who would be free to find the shortest route between any two points. Actually, of course, the result would be the very opposite of freedom. Boundaries are essential to freedom.

As regards moral freedom, the sphere of human behavior with which the Ten Commandments are concerned, it is much to be desired that these fences be accepted voluntarily—indeed, that they be built by the person himself and installed in his own heart, mind, and will. These fences, then, essentially are *commitments*.

But I am deeply convinced that, say, the man who commits himself to one woman, saying in effect, "I will find happiness with this woman or else I will not find happiness at all"—I believe that this man is much more likely to find true marital and sexual happiness than is the fence-hating freedom lover who says, "In my quest for happiness, I reserve the right to form whatever relationship with whatever woman I choose."

Likewise, in other areas, here are some of my own commitment-fences as examples: "I will find my professional fulfillment as a college teacher or I will not find it at all." Or, even more specifically, "I will make it as a professor of religion at La Verne College or not at all."

Now this sort of commitment does not preclude the possibility that at some point I may have to face up to the reality of the situation and confess, "That fence was a mistake; it is set at the wrong place; it will be necessary to reposition it at another spot." But this sober and thoughtful repositioning of bad fences is a far cry from the attitude that would renounce fences altogether—as it is also from the person making pseudo commitments who, in the very act of positioning fences, is also contemplating the possibility that they can be moved whenever the fancy strikes.

Neither those who hate fences nor those who play around with them are free people. Indeed, their idea of freedom would stand a ghost of a chance of working only if they were the only person around—and in a completely unstructured universe. In truth, such freedom would be workable only if one happened also to be God (not a god, but *the* Lord God Almighty and that before the creation, at which time he set some commitment-fences even for himself). And sad to say, a fenceless lover of freedom acts as though this is just who he thinks he is.

If, then, the wisdom with which one sets his individual commitment-fences determines whether his life is to be that of a free man on the one hand or a lost wanderer and/or slave on the other, it behooves him to get all the help and insight available.

The early Hebrews believed that in the Ten Commandments, God himself (the one who created men and their world and who certainly should know more about what makes for their freedom than does anyone else around) had offered to help them set their fences so as to insure maximum freedom.

Perhaps you do not buy the idea that there is a God who could or did help mankind in this way. In such case, consider that for over three thousand years now, myriads of men, representing a great variety of times, nations, cultures, and stations, have accepted these fences as defining their own "freedom run." These fences have been given the most thorough field test of any system ever devised. And from the millions who have tried them comes the mighty testimony: "Within these fences lies the freedom to live as men! With God's help, set your fences, and be free!"

More Big Laughs from SIGNET

☐ **IT'S A ZIGGY WORLD** by Tom Wilson. (#Q6809—95¢)

☐ **LIFE IS JUST A BUNCH OF ZIGGY'S** by Tom Wilson.
(#Y8450—$1.25)

☐ **PLANTS ARE SOME OF MY FAVORITE PEOPLE** by Tom Wilson. (#Y8055—$1.25)

☐ **ZIGGY'S OF THE WORLD UNITE!** by Tom Wilson.
(#Y7800—$1.25)

☐ **PETS ARE FRIENDS YOU LIKE WHO LIKE YOU RIGHT BACK** by Tom Wilson. (#Y8264—$1.25)

☐ **AL JAFFEE BLOWS HIS MIND** by Al Jaffee. (#Y6759—$1.25)

☐ **AL JAFFEE BOMBS AGAIN** by Al Jaffee. (#W9273—$1.50)

☐ **AL JAFFEE DRAWS A CROWD** by Al Jaffee. (#W9275—$1.50)

☐ **AL JAFFEE'S NEXT BOOK** by Al Jaffee. (#W9260—$1.50)

☐ **THE LOCKHORNS #1—"WHAT'S THE GARBAGE DOING ON THE STOVE?"** by Bill Hoest. (#Y8166—$1.25)

☐ **THE LOCKHORNS #2—"LORETTA, THE MEATLOAF IS MOVING!"** by Bill Hoest. (#Y8167—$1.25)

☐ **THE LOCKHORNS #4—"IS THIS THE STEAK OR THE CHARCOAL?"** by Bill Hoest. (#Y8475—$1.25)*

* Price slightly higher in Canada

Buy them at your local

bookstore or use coupon

on next page for ordering.

SIGNET Peanuts Books by Charles M. Schulz

☐ **CHARLIE BROWN'S ALL STARS** (#Y7688—$1.25)

☐ **A CHARLIE BROWN CHRISTMAS** (#Y7206—$1.25)

☐ **A CHARLIE BROWN THANKSGIVING** (#Y6885—$1.25)

☐ **IT WAS A SHORT SUMMER, CHARLIE BROWN**
(#Y7958—$1.25)

☐ **IT'S A MYSTERY, CHARLIE BROWN** (#Y8238—$1.25)

☐ **IT'S THE GREAT PUMPKIN, CHARLIE BROWN**
(#Y7809—$1.25)

☐ **PLAY IT AGAIN, CHARLIE BROWN** (#W9217—$1.50)

☐ **THERE'S NO TIME FOR LOVE, CHARLIE BROWN**
(#Y6886—$1.25)

☐ **YOU'RE IN LOVE, CHARLIE BROWN** (#Y8175—$1.25)

ith only her small pink face visible above the yellow blan-
t that swaddled her.

The sight of Joe, her handsome masculine husband, set-
d in a rocking chair with that tiny, precious speck of hu-
anity cradled against his chest moved Meg to quick, sweet
ars.

"Postpartum blues?"

She shook her head. "The opposite. I'm happier than I
ver dreamed possible."

The baby stirred, and Joe's large hand gently massaged
r tiny back. "Are you sorry your parents didn't stay for
e party afterward?"

It was an old pain but one Meg had learned to bear.
They came," she said. "It's a step in the right direction."

Joe's love during their five years of marriage had ban-
hed all the shadows from Meg's life. She wasn't foolish
nough to think that Krissie's existence would do the same
r the Lindstroms, but Meg hoped her parents would, in
me, allow some happiness back into their own lives in the
erson of their new granddaughter. Her sister, Kay, would
ways live in her heart, but Meg no longer felt the need to
ve in her shadow.

Marriage to Joe had brought with it a happiness that
eemed to grow daily. The security she'd found with him
reed her to take on professional challenges she'd never
ared before. While her decision to refuse credit for the
eople magazine spread on Huntington Kendall had baf-
led Joe, she knew she had made the right decision. Hunt
ad still garnered the attention he deserved, and seeing his
areer skyrocket had brought her tremendous pleasure. Meg
hen set out to see if she could make it on her own.

Slowly, she'd accumulated credits in prestigious publica-
ions. Sometimes the progress seemed slower than the sands
f time. Word began to spread, and her work was exhibited
n galleries on two coasts and in Rome; finally, two years
go, her series on *Vanishing America* was optioned by *Time-
ife Books*. While she wasn't a household name yet, her

reputation was growing, and her horizons were as limitless as her capacity to love and be loved.

Joe had taught her how to dream, and she had managed to make those very dreams come true.

Joseph Alessio, however, *had* become a household name—at last.

Fire's Lady, the book Meg inspired, had topped the *New York Times* best-seller list for sixteen weeks. A miniseries for HBO had garnered enough interest in the true identity of Angelique Moreau that Joe finally stepped out from behind his female pseudonym and into the limelight he deserved. His first nonfiction work was due on the bookshelves in two weeks, and his palms still grew sweaty each time he thought about it.

Thanks to Meg's emotional support, he had finally been able to unravel his nineteen months in Vietnam and weave his experience into the rich and tangled tapestry of experiences of other men who had been less fortunate than he. Advance word in the trades said that *In the Midnight Hour* was the definitive work on the Vietnam experience. More importantly, it had helped Joe put his fears to rest.

The baby in his arms yawned. Her eyes opened. They were a startling deep green, the same eyes he saw in his mirror every morning when he shaved. Proof that his blood and the blood of all who had come before him ran through Kristen's veins, giving him an immortality that his books would never achieve. The sense of family, of continuity he had sought in his work, was encompassed now in the woman who sat by his side and the child in his arms.

Kristen, however, was totally oblivious to such heavy thoughts. She knew about sleep and comfort; she also knew about food, and her hungry mouth turned and sought sustenance.

"Oh, no, little one," he said with a laugh as she took his pinky in her mouth and suckled. "This is your mother's job."

He stood up, and Meg settled herself down in the rocking chair, unbuttoned her blouse and released one breast from the confines of her nursing bra. She held out her hands for the baby, and Joe watched as the infant unerringly found the nipple and began blissfully nursing.

Outside it was dark and cold, but inside, in that magical room where he and Meg had watched *Casablanca* one night long ago and fallen in love, his wife and daughter were bathed in the amber glow of the firelight, warmed by the glow of his love for them both.

He knelt before Meg and rested one hand against her cheek, offering the other to Kristen, who grasped at his pinky with a plump fist, misjudging it each time. The best things life had to offer were within the reach of his arms.

"Joe?" Meg's voice was tender. "What are you thinking?"

He swallowed hard against the lump in his throat, then smiled at his wife. "I was just thinking it's time we watched *Casablanca* again."

"Ah, Joseph," she said. "You're still a hopeless romantic."

She smiled at him. He smiled back. The baby found his pinky and held it tight.

Reality.

He loved it.

Harlequin American Romance

COMING NEXT MONTH

#141 THE STRAIGHT GAME by Rebecca Flanders

E. J. Wiley looked at the man across her desk—one Colby James.
He claimed to be an itinerant sailor and dockworker.
Honoraria Fitzgerald called him her long-lost son and heir to her
San Francisco fortune. E.J. didn't know who was right—she only
knew he was her fantasy.

#142 WINTER MAGIC by Margaret St. George

Even as Teddi watched the icy flakes falling from the warmth of
the ski lodge, her drying throat constricted her breathing. It had
been six years since she'd seen her family and friends—and
snow. But it wasn't until her eyes lit on the indomitable
Grant Sterling that she knew returning to Vail was her greatest
mistake.

#143 A FAMILY TO CHERISH by Cathy Gillen Thacker

More than anything Christy Shannon wanted this family.
Orphaned and now widowed, she couldn't understand why her
husband had run away and denied his relatives. Until she visited
the Texas ranch and met his brother, Jake. Jake opened his
home to Christy, but he swore she'd never uncover the shocking
incident that was the brothers' secret.

#144 A CLASS ABOVE by Carolyn Thornton

Squawking roadside chickens, rundown pickups and circling
buzzards. It wasn't exactly what she expected when she
accepted the challenge of this hitchhiking contest. For risk was
Tara Jefferson's middle name. But little did she know that when
she hitched a ride with pilot Marcus Landry he'd be taking her
on the adventure of a lifetime.

You can keep this one plus 4 free novels